God's Blueprint for Bible Prophecy

KAY ARTHUR

HARVEST HOUSE™PUBLISHERS

EUGENE, OREGON

The New Inductive Study Series
GOD'S BLUEPRINT FOR BIBLE PROPHECY
Copyright © 1995 by Precept Ministries International
Published by Harvest House Publishers
Eugene, Oregon 97402

Library of Congress Cataloging-in-Publication Data
Arthur, Kay, 1933–
    God's blueprint for Bible prophecy / Kay Arthur.
      p. cm. — (The new inductive study series)
    ISBN 0-7369-0802-1
    1. Bible. O.T. Daniel—Prophecies—Study and teaching.
    I. Title. II. Series: Arthur, Kay, 1933–
    The new inductive study series.
BS1556.A7 1995
224'.5015'07—dc20

95-9662
CIP

Printed in the United States of America.

05 06 07 08 09 10 / BP-CF / 10 9 8 7 6 5 4

CONTENTS

∾∾∾∾

How to Get Started...

Reading directions is sometimes difficult and seldom enjoyable! Most often you just want to get started, and only if all else fails will you read the instructions. I understand, but please don't approach this study that way! These brief instructions are a vital part of getting started on the right foot—they will help you immensely.

FIRST

As you study the book of Daniel, you will need four things in addition to this book:

1. A Bible that you are willing to mark in. An ideal Bible for this purpose is *The New Inductive Study Bible (NISB)*. The *NISB* is in a single-column text format with large, easy-to-read type which is ideal for marking. Also, the margins of the text are wide for note-taking. (The charts and maps in this study guide are taken from the *NISB*.) The *NISB* has instructions for studying each book of the Bible, but does not contain commentary on the text, nor is it compiled from a particular theological stance. Its purpose is to teach you how to discern truth for yourself through the inductive method of study.

Whatever Bible you use, just know you will need to mark in it—marking is essential to our method of study.

2. A fine-point, four-color ballpoint pen or various colored fine-point pens that you can use to write in your Bible (office supply stores will have these).

3. Colored pencils or an eight-color Pentel pencil.

4. A composition book or a notebook for working on your assignments and recording your insights.

SECOND

1. As you study the book of Daniel, you will be given specific instructions for each day. These assignments should take you 25 to 30 minutes a day (but if you spend more time than this you will increase your intimacy with the Word of God and the God of the Word!).

If you are doing this study within the framework of a class and find the lessons too intense, simply do what you can. To do a little is better than to do nothing; don't be all-or-nothing when it comes to Bible study.

Remember, any time you get into the Word of God you enter into more intensive warfare with the devil (our enemy). Why? Every piece of the Christian's armor is related to the Word of God. And our main offensive weapon is the sword of the Spirit, which is the Word of God. The enemy wants you to have a dull sword. But you don't have to!

2. As you read each chapter, train yourself to ask the "5 W's and an H": who, what, when, where, why, and how. Asking these questions will help you see exactly what the Word of God is saying. When you interrogate the text with the 5 W's and an H, you ask questions like:

a. **What** is the chapter about?
b. **Who** are the main characters?
c. **When** does this event or teaching take place?
d. **Where** does this happen?

e. **Why** is this being done or said?

f. **How** did this happen?

3. The "when" of events or teachings is very important and should be marked in an easily recognizable way in your Bible. I do this by putting a clock (like the one shown here) 🕐 in the margin of my Bible beside the verse where the time phrase occurs. You may also want to underline or color the references to time in one specific color.

4. You will be given certain key words to mark throughout the book of Daniel. This is the purpose of the colored pencils and pen. Developing the habit of marking your Bible in this way will make a significant difference in the effectiveness of your study and how much you remember.

A **key word** is an important word that is used by the author repeatedly in order to convey his message to his reader. Certain key words will show up throughout the book; others will be concentrated in specific chapters or segments of the book. When you mark a key word, you should also mark its synonyms (words that mean the same thing in the context) and pronouns (*he, his, she, her, it, we, they, us, our, you, their, them*) in the same way.

Marking words for easy identification can be done with colors or symbols or a combination of colors and symbols. However, colors are easier to distinguish than symbols. If I use symbols, I keep them very simple. For example, I color *repent* yellow but put a red diagram around it: repent . The symbol conveys the meaning of the word.

When I mark the members of the Godhead (which I do not always mark), I color each word yellow. But I also use a purple pen and mark the Father with a triangle: God, symbolizing the Trinity. I mark the Son this way: Jesus, and the Holy Spirit like this: Spirit .

Your color-coding system for marking key words should be standard throughout your Bible so that when you look at the pages of your Bible, you can see instantly where a key word is used. When you start marking key words, it is easy to forget how you are marking them. I recommend using the bottom portion of the perforated card at the back of this book to write the key words on. Color-code the words and then use the card as a bookmark. You may want to make one bookmark for words you are marking throughout your Bible and a different one for the specific book of the Bible you are studying.

5. A chart called DANIEL AT A GLANCE is located at the end of this study. As you complete your study of each chapter, record the main theme of that chapter under the appropriate chapter number. The main theme of a chapter is what the chapter deals with the most. It may be an event or a particular subject or teaching.

If you fill out the DANIEL AT A GLANCE chart as you progress through the study, you will have a complete synopsis of the book when you finish. If you have *The New Inductive Study Bible,* you will find this chart in your Bible. By recording your chapter themes there, you'll always have them for ready reference.

6. Always begin your study with prayer. As you do your part to handle the Word of God accurately, remember that the Bible is a divinely inspired book. The words you are reading are truth, given to you by God so you can know Him and His ways more intimately. These truths are divinely revealed.

> For to us God revealed them through the Spirit; for the Spirit searches all things, even the depths of God. For who among men

> knows the thoughts of a man except the spirit
> of the man which is in him? Even so the
> thoughts of God no one knows except the
> Spirit of God (1 Corinthians 2:10,11).

Therefore, ask God to reveal His truth to you as He leads and guides you into all truth. He will, if you will ask.

7. Each day when you finish your lesson, meditate on what you learned. Ask your heavenly Father how you should live in light of the truths you have just studied. At times, depending on how God has spoken to you through His Word, you might want to record these "Lessons for Life" (LFLs) in your Bible next to the text you studied. Simply put "LFL" in the margin of your Bible, and then, as briefly as possible, record the lesson for life that you want to remember.

THIRD

This study is set up so that you have an assignment for every day of the week. If you work through your study this way, you will find it more profitable than doing a week's study in one sitting. Pacing yourself this way allows time for thinking through what you learn and puts you in the Word *daily!*

The seventh day of each week has several features that are different than the other days. These features are designed to aid group discussion; however, they are also profitable if you are studying this book on your own. The "seventh day" is whatever day in the week you choose to finish your week's study. On this day, you will find a verse or two to memorize and STORE IN YOUR HEART. This will help you focus on a major truth or truths covered in your study that week.

To assist those using the material in a Sunday school class or a group Bible study, there are QUESTIONS FOR DISCUSSION OR INDIVIDUAL STUDY. Even if you are not doing this study with someone else, answering these questions will contribute greatly to your study.

If you are in a group, be sure every member of the class—including the teacher—supports his or her answers and insights *from the Bible text itself.* Then you will be handling the Word of God accurately. Always examine your insights by carefully observing the text to see what it *says.* Then, before you decide what the passage of Scripture *means,* make sure you interpret it in light of its context. Scripture never contradicts Scripture. If it ever seems to contradict the rest of the Word of God, you can be certain that something is being taken out of context. If you come to a passage that is difficult to understand, reserve your interpretations for a time when you can study the passage in greater depth.

The primary purpose of the THOUGHT FOR THE WEEK section is to share with you what I consider to be an important element for that week of study. I have included it for your evaluation and, hopefully, your edification. This section will help you walk in light of what you learned.

Books in The New Inductive Study Series are survey courses. If you want to do a more in-depth study of a particular book of the Bible, I suggest you do a Precept Upon Precept Bible study course on that book. You may obtain more information on these courses by contacting Precept Ministries International at 800-763-8280, visiting our website at www.precept.org, or filling out and mailing the response card at the back of this book.

SPECIAL NOTE TO LEADERS

If you are planning on leading this NISS study in a group setting, you may find it valuable to also work through the inductive course I have written on the book of

Daniel called *In God's Plan...What Is Happening on Earth?* Some adults have also studied an inductive course I wrote for teens called *Daniels for the 1990s*. These studies take about five hours a week. I also have lecture tapes which accompany each lesson to enhance and expand what you have seen on your own as you worked through the lesson. The use of the lecture tapes (available in either audio or video format) is optional.

In addition to my teaching tapes we offer leader guides that are designed to help anyone who plans to lead a group discussion on either of these studies.

If you are interested in these materials, call Precept Ministries International, Information Services at 800-763-8280.

DANIEL

INTRODUCTION

∾∾∾∾

If you love prophecy or are curious (maybe even nervous) about the future, you need to familiarize yourself with the book of Daniel, God's blueprint for prophecy. And in the midst of all its incredible prophecies that take us to the time of the end, Daniel gives us more than God's blueprint for prophecy! The book of Daniel provides us with someone we can pattern our lives after—a man who receives accolades in heaven's court and who is referred to as "a man of high esteem."

It is my prayer that your passion will be to live as a person of high esteem in the eyes of God and the angelic host who serve Him. I pray that you will come to know Him as *El Elyon*, the Most High God who does according to His will in His army and among the inhabitants of the earth. In that knowledge and the relationship it brings, you, my friend, will find the peace which passes all understanding and which is able to hold you in the darkest of nights.

Such knowledge, Beloved, should enable you to be strong and do exploits...

DETERMINED TO BE A "DANIEL"

DAY ONE

Read through Daniel 1 today to familiarize yourself with the historical setting of this book. Also look for any reference to time and mark or color it in a distinctive way. As suggested in the instructions at the beginning of the book, you may want to use the symbol of a clock ⏰ to mark words or phrases referring to time.

When you finish your reading, write down the names of the main characters mentioned in this chapter in your notebook. (You should stop now and take the time to learn how to spell Nebuchadnezzar and Jehoiakim.)

DAY TWO

Read through Daniel 1 again today. (If you read the chapter aloud every day you will find you grasp it more quickly and remember it more easily.)

Note the names of the two kings and the kingdoms over which each rules. Observe what one king does to the other and the result of this action. Record your insights in your notebook.

DAY THREE

Today, read Daniel 1 again and mark two key words, each in a distinctive way: *Daniel* and *God*. Be sure you remember to mark any pronouns that refer to them also. These are two key words you'll want to mark throughout the book of Daniel. The other key words you'll mark are specific to chapters or sections of the book. I'll give you those words as we progress throughout the book. (If you need help in understanding how to mark key words, go back and read the instructions related to key words in the "How to Get Started" section at the beginning of this book.)

Read 2 Chronicles 36:1-8 and look for the names of the two kings you saw mentioned in Daniel 1. If you observe any new insights on these kings, record these in your notebook with what you noted yesterday. Look for the names of these kings on the chart THE RULERS AND PROPHETS OF DANIEL'S TIME on page 19 and note the year these events take place.

DAY FOUR

Read Daniel 1 again. Observe carefully all the chapter tells you about Daniel by noting where you marked his name as a key word yesterday. In your notebook, set aside several pages to record what you learn about Daniel as you work through this book. You could call the list PROFILE ON DANIEL. Now, list what you see about him from this chapter. Remember to note the chapter and verse reference to each insight as you move through the book. For example, your list might look something like the one on page 20.

THE RULERS AND PROPHETS OF DANIEL'S TIME

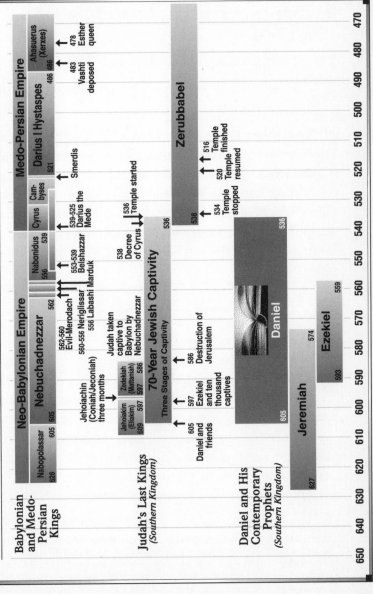

Babylonian and Medo-Persian Kings

Neo-Babylonian Empire

| | Medo-Persian Empire |

Nabopolassar 626 – 605

Nebuchadnezzar 605 – 562

562–560 Evil-Merodach
560–556 Neriglissar
556 Labashi Marduk

Nabonidus 556 – 539
553–539 Belshazzar

Cyrus 539

Cambyses 539–525 Darius the Mede

Smerdis 521

Darius I Hystaspes

486 Vashti deposed 483
Ahasuerus (Xerxes) 486
478 Esther queen

Judah's Last Kings *(Southern Kingdom)*

Jehoiakim (Eliakim) 609 597
Jehoiachin (Coniah/Jeconiah) three months
Zedekiah (Mattaniah) 597 586

Judah taken captive to Babylon by Nebuchadnezzar

70-Year Jewish Captivity
Three Stages of Captivity

605 Daniel and friends
597 Ezekiel and ten thousand captives
586 Destruction of Jerusalem
538 Decree of Cyrus
536 Temple started
536

538
534 Temple stopped
520 Temple resumed
516 Temple finished

Zerubbabel

Daniel and His Contemporary Prophets *(Southern Kingdom)*

Jeremiah 627 – 574

Ezekiel 593 – 559

Daniel 605 – 536

650 640 630 620 610 600 590 580 570 560 550 540 530 520 510 500 490 480 470

PROFILE ON DANIEL

1. taken captive when Nebuchadnezzar besieged Jerusalem (1:1-6)

2. from Judah—of the sons of Judah (1:6)

3. selected to enter the king of Babylon's personal service (1:5)

Remember, Daniel was called a "man of high esteem." The English transliteration of the Hebrew word for esteem is *chamudah,** which literally means "desirable" or "precious." Keep this in mind as you study Daniel's life. Look for things which caused him to be recognized as a man who was precious to God. If you, too, desire to be a man or a woman of high esteem in God's eyes, Daniel is your model!

DAY FIVE

One goal of this study is to learn about God's character and ways. Therefore, read Daniel 1 again. (You're really going to know this chapter, aren't you!) As you read today, carefully observe every reference to God you marked two days ago. If you see any references you missed, mark them.

You have begun a list of all you are learning on Daniel; now begin a list on all you'll learn about God. Be sure to leave several pages in your notebook for your list, and remember to note the chapter and verse for each insight.

---

* From time to time we will look at the definition of a word in Hebrew. Since the Old Testament was originally written in Hebrew, sometimes it is helpful to go back to the Hebrew to see the original meaning of the word. We will always use the English transliteration of the Hebrew alphabet—that is, the equivalent English letters according to pronunciation. There are many study tools to help you if you like to do this type of digging. One excellent book that will teach you how to do this type of in-depth study is *How to Study Your Bible* (Harvest House Publishers).

From what you learn today by compiling your list, answer the question, "Does God change?" How can the insights you are gaining help you live your life day in and day out? Think about it! If you find any LFLs—Lessons for Life—record them in your notebook (and in the margin of your Bible if you want). You may want to refer back to "How to Get Started" to refresh your memory on LFLs.

As I read through the Old Testament and see something that God does, I put a triangle in the margin and color it yellow. Then, beside the triangle, I write down what God did. For example, next to Daniel 1:2, I would print: $\triangle$ "God delivers kings into the hands of an enemy." If you make notes like this as you read through your Bible, you'll have a permanent record of what God is like and of what He is able to do. You may not always understand the action, but you'll have it written down for a future time.*

DAY SIX

Today you need to read—you guessed it—Daniel 1 one last time.

When you finish your study today, record the theme of Daniel 1 on the DANIEL AT A GLANCE chart on page 126. (If someone asked you what Daniel 1 is about, what would you say? That's the theme! Once you discern the theme, reduce the thought to as few words as possible using words the Bible uses.)

Now think about all you've learned this week—just from observing the text! What do you see from Daniel's life that can be an example to you? Stop and think about it.

---

* If the margins in your Bible aren't wide enough, you might want to pray about getting a *New Inductive Study Bible*. It's available in the NAS version at your local Christian bookstore.

Circumstances which appear awful may be part of God's greater plan

How would you have responded if you were in Daniel's position?

What do you learn about God from this first chapter? How can what you observe be applied to your life?

Discuss what you've learned with the Lord in prayer. You might want to write out your prayer in your notebook.

He allowed defeat, Daniel could rely on Him

DAY SEVEN

 Store in your heart: Daniel 1:8.
Read and discuss: Daniel 1.

QUESTIONS FOR DISCUSSION OR INDIVIDUAL STUDY

∽ What do you learn from Daniel 1 about the timing of the events? Or, to put it another way, "What is the historical setting of the book of Daniel?" Discuss what you learned from your study this week as you observed the text and looked at the chart THE RULERS AND PROPHETS OF DANIEL'S TIME.

∽ How does understanding the historical setting of Daniel help you appreciate Daniel's situation?

∽ What do you learn about Daniel from this chapter?

a. Discuss the insights on your Daniel list.

b. What do you see in Daniel's life that you can apply to your own? What does he do that you need to be doing? Is there an attitude in him that you need to have?

c. What do you learn about Daniel that explains why one of God's angels later refers to him as a "man of high esteem"?

∿ What do you learn about God from this chapter?

   a. In relation to what happened to the king of Judah

   b. In relation to Daniel

∿ From what you just discussed, what do you conclude?

∿ Do you think God is able to do the same things today?

THOUGHT FOR THE WEEK

Daniel found himself taken captive by a man who was a heathen—a man who didn't know God and who had no respect for the holy vessels of God. He found himself a hostage in a strange land. And whatever this 15-year-old had dreamed his future would hold, it was shattered. He was no longer free. He was held captive by a man who did not care personally for him or for his God. And, since Daniel was chosen to serve in the king's court, it is likely that he was made a eunuch (was castrated).

Yet Daniel did not become bitter or question his God; he continued to faithfully serve God. He did not break God's laws and defile himself with the king's choice food and wine. It seems that only three of the other captives stood with him in that decision.

Daniel was firm in his faith, but never disrespectful to those who did not share his faith, to those who ruled over him. And the God who was watching took notice and moved on his behalf.

O Beloved, may we be "Daniels" for the Lord. No matter the circumstances of our lives, may we be faithful to the One who is over every circumstance—the One who is rightly called the Most High God.

GOD'S BLUEPRINT
OF THE FUTURE

〰〰〰〰

DAY ONE

Read Daniel 2 today and mark every reference to Daniel.

DAY TWO

Now we'll begin to look at an overview of Daniel 2. Read Daniel 2:1-24 to find the setting of this chapter. As you read, ask the 5 W's and an H: who, what, when, where, why, and how. For example, ask:

a. Who or what is this segment of this chapter about?
   D. interprets N. prophetic dream
b. Who are the main characters? What does the text tell you about them?
   N. D. S, M, A
c. What is happening?
   N. can't sleep
d. When is it happening?
   2nd yr. of his reign
e. Where is it happening?
   Babylon
f. Why is it happening?
   Show God as God
g. How is it going to be handled? By whom?
   D. rely on God to interpret dreams
   + save his life

25

Record your insights in your notebook. Be sure to note how the king intends to solve his problem and how Daniel intends to solve his problem.

DAY THREE

Read Daniel 2:1-35. Be certain to concentrate on Nebuchadnezzar's dream.

Now, on the sketch of the statue on page 27, record what you learn about the dream. Only note what you learn in Daniel 2:1-35! Draw a stone on the diagram where you think it should go.

Record in your notebook what Daniel 2:25-35 is all about. Be as brief as possible.

Rock strikes statues feet + all blown away

DAY FOUR

Read Daniel 2:36-49. Record any new insights you gain on the statue sketch. Getting the details of this dream correct is important because every other prophecy in Daniel fits into the overall scheme of this dream.

When you read Daniel 2:36-49, did you notice any references to numerical order (third, fourth, etc.)? If so, you might want to circle these numbers and observe how many kingdoms there will be before the stone crushes the statue. Also, see if the text tells you how many kingdoms there will be after the stone crushes the statue. Note if the text tells you how reliable this interpretation is.

You may want to draw the statue in your notebook, including your insights on what each part represents.

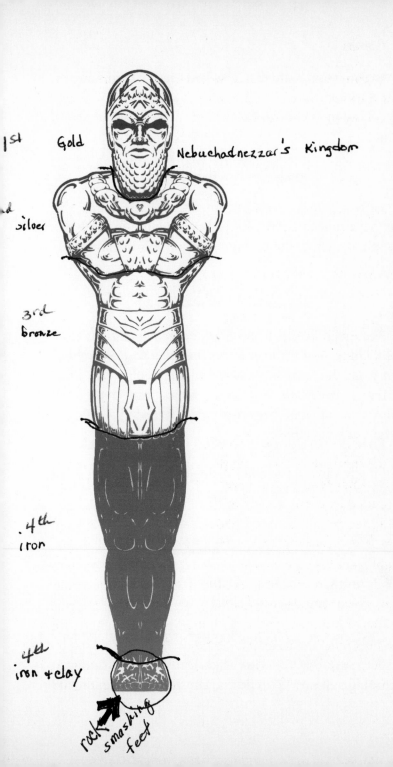

1st Gold

Nebuchadnezzar's Kingdom

2nd silver

3rd bronze

4th iron

4th iron + clay

rock smashing feet

Having your sketch there will let you keep all your notes on Daniel in one place.

Record in your notebook what Daniel 2:36-49 is about.

dream's interpretation

DAY FIVE

Reread Daniel 2, marking any references to Daniel you may have missed earlier. Record any further insights you gain on Daniel on the list you've begun in your notebook.

DAY SIX

Now, read Daniel 2 and mark every reference to God. Then add to your list in your notebook all you learn about God from this chapter. It is most enlightening and comforting! If you want to keep the major things you learn about God at your fingertips, also record these in the margin of your Bible.

Record any LFLs from chapter 2 that you see.

Finally, discern the main theme of Daniel 2 and record it on the DANIEL AT A GLANCE chart (page 126).

DAY SEVEN

 Store in your heart: Daniel 2:20,21.
Read and discuss: Daniel 2:17-49.

QUESTIONS FOR DISCUSSION OR INDIVIDUAL STUDY

∾ If someone were to ask what Daniel 2 is about, what would you say? What do you consider the main theme?

D. interprets N's dream. 4 powerful kingdoms will fall, conquered by God's eternal kingdom

∿ Why does King Nebuchadnezzar order all the "wise men" of Babylon to be put to death? *can't tell him his dream*

life lesson ∿ What does Daniel do when he receives the news of his impending death? (Be specific.) *He, S, A, M all pray for wisdom*

∿ If you have a whiteboard (or blackboard) in your classroom, have someone in the class draw the statue and note what the king dreamed as the class shares.

∿ What is the interpretation of this dream? *4 kingdoms, will rise, all will fall*

   a. How many kingdoms are represented? *4*

   b. What do you learn about the fourth kingdom? (Cover every detail of verses 40-44.)

life lesson *disunity, overthrown*

   c. Remembering the context, what do the ten toes represent? Did anyone see any relationship between the ten toes in verses 42, 43, and 44? *: 10 tribes of Israel*

split allegiance *"vulnerable"*

   d. Where does the stone strike the statue? What happens to the statue as a result? *feet, it falls*

   e. What events happen after the stone strikes the statue? What kingdom endures and for how long? *kingdom falls God's, forever*

   f. Who does the stone represent? *Jesus*

   g. According to the text, how sure is this interpretation? *certain*

∿ What do you learn about Daniel from this chapter that would later cause an angel to refer to him as a "man of high esteem"? *gives God credit, gives S, M.A credit*

   a. Have you or are you facing a situation similar to the one Daniel is facing in this chapter?

   b. How is Daniel an example for you?

∾ What do you learn about God from Daniel 2? What
does this mean to you regarding your life experiences?

dependable, never failing

THOUGHT FOR THE WEEK

God rules. He is sovereign. He is the One who changes
the times and the epochs, who removes and establishes
kings. Because He is Alpha and Omega, the beginning and
the end, He knows the beginning from the end; therefore,
if you want to know what the future holds, you need to
seek the wisdom of the One who holds the future in His
hands.

When you find yourself threatened by people who
claim to hold your future—even your life—in their hands,
remember who is on the throne. God never vacates it. So
run to Him, Beloved, and ask Him what you are to do.
Then wait and listen carefully—He will speak. Cling to
what He tells you in the stillness of your heart. And
remember, the stone is coming—His kingdom will be the
only one that will endure forever.

DETERMINED TO BURN RATHER THAN BOW

DAY ONE

Read Daniel 3 and simply note the content of this chapter. As you read, mark any references to Daniel.

DAY TWO

The first six chapters of Daniel are in chronological order. So, at this point in your study of Daniel, it would be helpful to get an overview of the various world kingdoms which ruled from the time of Daniel through the time of the Lord Jesus Christ's death, burial, resurrection, and the destruction of Jerusalem in A.D. 70.

Today and tomorrow we'll look at two charts that will help you gain this overview. THE RULERS AND PROPHETS OF DANIEL'S TIME is on page 19. As you look at this chart, note under the "Babylonian and Medo-Persian Kings" the year that Nebuchadnezzar began his reign. Then look under "Judah's Last Kings" at the "70-Year Jewish Captivity" section and note the year Daniel and his friends were taken captive. Record this year next to Daniel 1:1 in the margin of your Bible.

Daniel 1:1 says "in the third year of the reign of Jehoiakim king of Judah." The chart says Jehoiakim began his reign in 609 B.C., which may seem like "the fourth year of the reign of Jehoiakim." Although Jehoiakim's reign officially began in 609 B.C., counting the time he had reigned when Nebuchadnezzar besieged Jerusalem in 605 B.C., Jehoiakim was only in his third full year of actually sitting on the throne.

Now read Daniel 2:1 and note when the events of Daniel 2 occur. Record the year in the margin of your Bible.

DAY THREE

Today study the WORLD KINGDOMS FROM DANIEL'S TIME ON chart on the next page and note the number of world kingdoms from Babylon (counting Babylon) to the time of Jesus Christ. Memorize these in chronological order.

Now read Daniel 2:36-45 again. What do you think the names of the kingdoms in Daniel 2 are? How do you know the name of the first kingdom? What followed in history according to the chart WORLD KINGDOMS FROM DANIEL'S TIME ON? Add these names to the sketch of the statue you worked on last week.

DAY FOUR

Read Daniel 3:1-7. Examine this segment of Daniel 3 in the light of the 5 W's and an H:

1. What is this part of the chapter about?

2. Who are the main characters, and what do you learn about them?

WORLD KINGDOMS FROM DANIEL'S TIME ON

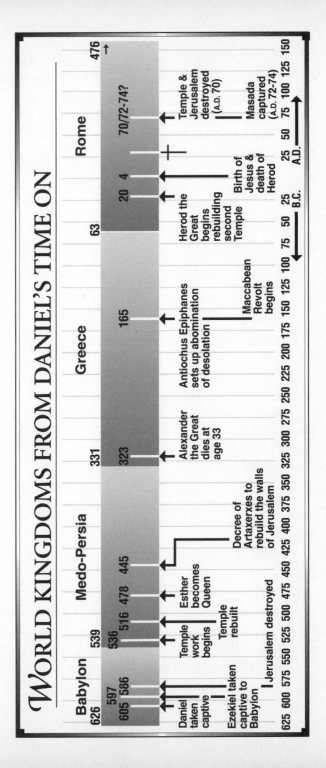

3. When are the events of Daniel 3:1-7 taking place? (Even if you don't find any mention of specific time, think about what happened in Daniel 1 and 2 to help you define the order of events.)

4. What are the people to do?

5. Why do you think the king is having them do this?

6. What is the image made of?

7. How does this image compare with Nebuchadnezzar's dream and the statue in that dream?

8. What do you think Nebuchadnezzar is doing or saying with the erection of this statue?

Record your insights in your notebook.

DAY FIVE

Read Daniel 3:1-18. Mark any reference to God.

Summarize the situation in Daniel 3:8-18 and record it in your notebook.

DAY SIX

Read Daniel 3:13-30. Mark every reference to God in 3:19-30.

Add to your list in your notebook what you learn about God from Daniel 3. Also, don't forget to record insights about God in the margin of your Bible for ready reference.

Do you see any LFLs? Write them in your notebook. Also list in your notebook everything you learn about Shadrach, Meshach, and Abed-nego.

Record the theme of Daniel 3 on the DANIEL AT A GLANCE chart.

DAY SEVEN

 Store in your heart: Daniel 3:17,18 or 28.
Read and discuss: Daniel 3:13-30; Exodus 20:1-6.

QUESTIONS FOR DISCUSSION OR INDIVIDUAL STUDY

∾ Why do you think King Nebuchadnezzar built the golden statue and dictated that everyone in his kingdom fall down and worship it?

a. Do you see any relationship between the king's actions and his dream and its interpretation as recorded in Daniel 2?

b. Discuss the four major world powers from the time of Daniel through the time of Christ. If the members of the class can give the names of the kingdoms in the order in which they rule from memory, have them do so. Otherwise have them look at the chart and recite the world powers. It would be good to review this list until the class knows them.

c. Which of these kingdoms did Daniel live under?

∾ How did Shadrach, Meshach, and Abed-nego respond to the king's edict? Why do you think they responded this way? Does the text tell us where Daniel is during this time? What does this tell you about Shadrach, Meshach, and Abed-nego?

∾ What is their condition as they are thrown into the furnace? What is their condition when they come out? What happens in the furnace?

～ Are these men willing to die even if God doesn't deliver them? Why? *B/c they love Him irregardless*

～ Are there some things in your life that you feel you can't compromise? What are they? To what extent are you willing to go to keep from compromising? Do you think you'll ever come to a situation like that of Shadrach, Meshach, and Abed-nego? Have you thought about what you would do? Is there anything in your life that you consider a compromise? How are you dealing with it before God? Why?

～ What do you learn from these young men that you can apply to your own life? *don't let pressure force you to compromise your conviction*

～ How did the lives of these men impact Nebuchadnezzar's life? Why? *stood up to, pointed out God's over-riding power*

～ What do you learn about God from this chapter? *He is faithful, our deliverer*

～ What did you record as the theme of this chapter?

THOUGHT FOR THE WEEK

The world would have us bow at its shrines, worship its gods. It would threaten the life, security, and future of those who don't follow. However, we are not to conform to this world nor be intimidated by it or its threats. The God who rules over kingdoms and their kings, who sets kings up and removes them, tells us we are to worship Him and Him alone. We are to have no other god! And we are to obey Him no matter the cost, no matter the raving and threats of the world. We are to vow in our hearts that we'll burn before we bow! Vow, Beloved, and then keep your vow to the Most High God.

HE RULES—HE'S THE MOST HIGH GOD

DAY ONE

Read through Daniel 4 to familiarize yourself with the content of the entire chapter. As you read, mark every reference to *the Most High (God)*,[1] which is one of the names for God. In the Hebrew this word is *El Elyon*, so mark it in the same way you mark other references to God. Also mark every reference to Daniel.

As you read, note who is speaking (or seems to be doing the writing) in this chapter. Clues to who is writing are in verses 4, 34, and 37.

Also add to your list in your notebook what you learn about Daniel from this chapter.

DAY TWO

Read Daniel 4:1-18. Record your insights using the 5 W's and an H in your notebook. Note who is talking, what they are talking about, etc.

DAY THREE

Read Daniel 4:19-27. Mark any references to time. Also give careful attention to the details of the interpretation of the dream. Note what the tree represents and what will happen to the tree and the stump. Then watch the switch of pronouns in reference to the stump and what you observe about "him." Carefully observe what Daniel tells the king will happen to him.

Record your observations in your notebook. Remember, the discipline of recording your insights will help you retain what you have read.

DAY FOUR

Read Daniel 4:28-37 and mark any reference to time. Once again examine this passage in light of the 5 W's and an H. Note how Nebuchadnezzar's dream is fulfilled and how he responds. Record your insights in your notebook.

DAY FIVE

Read through Daniel 4:19-37 again. This time, mark any reference to sin (*sins* and *iniquities*[2]). Note what Nebuchadnezzar's sins or iniquities might be. What is he to do in respect to his sins?

DAY SIX

Read Daniel 4 again and mark any references to God. List in your notebook everything you learn about God. You may also want to record your insights in the margin of chapter 4 in your Bible. When you finish, take a few minutes to go through these points one by one and thank God for what you are learning about Him and what this knowledge means to you in your daily life. Also record any LFLs that apply to you.

Record the theme of Daniel 4 on the DANIEL AT A GLANCE chart.

DAY SEVEN

 Store in your heart: Daniel 4:34,35.
Read and discuss: Daniel 4:19-37.

QUESTIONS FOR DISCUSSION OR INDIVIDUAL STUDY

∼ What is Nebuchadnezzar's dream this time? Have someone review the dream.

∼ What is the interpretation of the dream? What does it mean? Are there any indications as to time?

∼ What is Nebuchadnezzar's sin? How should he respond when it is pointed out to him? Does he? How do you know?

∼ When is the dream fulfilled and how?

∼ What happens to Nebuchadnezzar as a result of the dream?

∼ What does Nebuchadnezzar learn about God? What do you learn about God from this chapter?

∼ What does this mean to you? How does this affect the way you look at life?

∼ How can you incorporate what you learn about God in this chapter into your worship of Him?

THOUGHT FOR THE WEEK

God rules, beloved child of God. He rules over every created being—angelic and human. He is sovereign. Therefore, whatever God wants to do, He does. No one can stop Him; no one can hinder or keep Him from doing what He desires to do. This is why you and I can rest in the certainty of what He says through the apostle Paul in Romans 8:28-30: "And we know that God causes all things to work together for good to those who love God, to those who are called according to *His* purpose. For whom He foreknew, He also predestined *to become* conformed to the image of His Son, that He would be the firstborn among many brethren; and these whom He predestined, He also called; and these whom He called, He also justified; and these whom He justified, He also glorified."

Yes, God rules, and we can rest in the knowledge of His sovereignty when we know His character. What is the Most High God like? First John 4:8 tells us "God is love." John 10:28 tells us that God holds us in His hand. Therefore, no one can touch us, speak to us, or even look at us without His permission. Everything that comes into our lives is filtered through His fingers of love. And we have the assurance that God will use it for our good in order to conform us to the image of Jesus Christ. And when we see Him face-to-face, being like Jesus is all that will matter.

Don't be like Nebuchadnezzar, my friend. Recognize who the Most High God is, get to know Him intimately through His Word, and then think and live accordingly. What peace, what security He will bring to your life! He will take you through every storm and bring you through it without bitterness, filled with the sweet fragrance of the presence of Christ.

*H*AVE *Y*OU *R*EAD THE *H*ANDWRITING ON THE *W*ALL?

DAY ONE

Read through Daniel 5 to get an overview of the chapter. Mark every occurrence of *the Most High God* and mark any other references to God.

DAY TWO

Read Daniel 5:1-9 to get the setting of this chapter. Mark every reference to the king. In your notebook record the name of the king and list everything you learn about him from this text.

Refer to THE RULERS AND PROPHETS OF DANIEL'S TIME (page 19) and note what kingdom he rules over and what king he succeeds. Record this information with your notes.

DAY THREE

Read Daniel 5:1-9 again. Mark the word *vessels*.[3]

What was so serious about what Belshazzar and the others from his royal court were doing? Read Exodus 30:25-30; 2 Chronicles 36:5-7,11-21 (Chaldeans is another word for Babylonians); and Numbers 7:1. Mark every reference to the vessels (referred to as *utensils, treasures,* and/or *articles*[4] in these passages) and note what was to be done with them, why, and what happened to them. You might want to write these cross-references in the margin of your Bible next to Daniel 5:2,3. Cross-referencing helps you remember the location of a passage that sheds light on or correlates with the one you are studying. Cross-referencing is also very helpful when you do not have your study notes because your notes are right in your Bible! So write these cross-references in the margin of your Bible close to the appropriate text in Daniel.

DAY FOUR

Read Daniel 5:1-16. Mark every reference to Daniel. Then list in your notebook everything you learn about Daniel from this passage.

DAY FIVE

Read Daniel 5:17-31. Once again mark every reference to Daniel. Watch how Daniel responds to the king and how he explains the handwriting on the wall. Also note how his words come to pass.

Again, add all you learn about Daniel to your notebook list. When you finish, review your list. Think of Daniel as a role model and see what you can learn about his life.

DAY SIX

Today, work through one paragraph at a time. It won't take as long as you think! When you are finished, you'll be excited by all you've seen and your appreciation of God will be deepened!

First read Daniel 5:1,30,31. Now let's take another look at the historical context of this passage. Consult the chart THE RULERS AND PROPHETS OF DANIEL'S TIME (page 19) and note when Darius the Mede begins his rule over the Babylonians (who were conquered by the Medo-Persians at that time). Daniel 5 tells how old Darius was at the time. On the chart you will also see "Cyrus," who rules the Medo-Persian Empire at the same time as Darius. You may want to record this date in the margin of your Bible next to Daniel 5:31.

Now look at "Judah's Last Kings" and the section called the "70-Year Jewish Captivity." Notice the year of the destruction of Jerusalem, then the year of the decree of Cyrus. Also notice at what period in Daniel's life the events of Daniel 5 occurred.

Let's look at passages that tell us about Cyrus; they show the sovereignty of God. When we speak of God's sovereignty we are referring to the fact that God rules over all, just as Daniel 4:34,35 says. (Those were your STORE IN YOUR HEART verses last week!)

Read Isaiah 44:28–45:7. List in your notebook all God says about Cyrus and what he will do. This passage was written approximately 150 years *before* Cyrus was born. Isaiah prophesied from 739–681 B.C. (Remember, the calendar years go down in number until we come to A.D., the year of our Lord; then they begin going up.)

Now read 2 Chronicles 36:11-23. Note what you learn about Cyrus.

The Word of God is awesome, isn't it! It was given to us by an awesome God. What did you learn about Him this week? Record any new insights on your list in your notebook and put them in the margin of your Bible if you want.

Also record any LFLs that you see in chapter 5.

Record the theme of Daniel 5 on the DANIEL AT A GLANCE chart at the end of this book.

DAY SEVEN

Store in your heart: Isaiah 45:6,7.
Read and discuss: Daniel 5:17-31 and Isaiah 44:28–45:7.

QUESTIONS FOR DISCUSSION OR INDIVIDUAL STUDY

∾ If someone were to ask what Daniel 5 is about, how would you answer?

∾ Where does Daniel 5 fit historically?

a. Discuss what you learned about the historical setting of this chapter.

b. At what period in Daniel's life does this event occur?

c. What seems to be Daniel's status in the Babylonian kingdom at this time?

d. Who tells the king about Daniel? How is he described?

∾ What do you learn about the vessels from the temple? What is the significance of what Belshazzar does that night at his feast?

~ When Daniel is called in to read the handwriting on the wall, what does he point out to Belshazzar?

   a. What does Belshazzar need to see?

   b. What does Belshazzar already know? Yet, how does he act?

   c. What are the consequences of Belshazzar's actions? Would you consider this fair?

~ Look at all you have listed about God since you began your study of the book of Daniel.

   a. How does this chapter confirm some of the insights you recorded earlier about God?

   b. What did you learn about God in this week's study?

   c. How can you apply these truths to your life?

~ What's been happening in your life since you began your study five weeks ago?

THOUGHT FOR THE WEEK

There are lessons to be learned from history. As you have seen, history is really "His story," for God rules over the affairs of man. He is the one who establishes and removes kings. He is the one who tells us things before they come to pass that we might know that He is "the LORD, and there is no other, the One forming light and creating darkness, causing well-being and creating calamity...the Lord who does all these" (Isaiah 45:6b,7).

God, in His Word, has given us everything we need to know about Him. He shows us how He rules in the affairs of man and what He expects them to know and obey. When we don't live accordingly, we walk in pride, and God, in His own unique way with us, may have to say, as He did to Belshazzar, "Yet you...have not humbled your heart, even though you knew all this, but you have exalted yourself against the Lord of heaven...the God in whose hand are your life-breath and your ways, you have not glorified" (Daniel 5:22,23).

O Beloved, don't wait for the handwriting on the wall! Humble yourself under the mighty hand of God that He might exalt you in due time.

> For the LORD is a God of knowledge, and with Him actions are weighed....The LORD kills and makes alive; He brings down to Sheol and raises up. The LORD makes poor and rich; He brings low, He also exalts. He raises the poor from the dust, He lifts the needy from the ash heap to make them sit with nobles, and inherit a seat of honor; for the pillars of the earth are the LORD's, and He set the world on them. He keeps the feet of His godly ones, but the wicked ones are silenced in darkness; for not by might shall a man prevail. Those who contend with the LORD will be shattered; against them He will thunder in the heavens, the LORD will judge the ends of the earth; and He will give strength to His king, and will exalt the horn of His anointed (1 Samuel 2:3b,6-10).

𝒯EAR 𝒢OD—𝓗E'LL 𝒯AKE CARE OF THE LIONS

DAY ONE

Read Daniel 6 to familiarize yourself with the content of this chapter. Maybe you heard this story as a child; see how what you read compares with what you heard.

DAY TWO

Read Daniel 6:1-9 to see the setting of this chapter as well as the setup!

When you finish reading this passage, examine it in the light of the 5 W's and an H and record your observations in your notebook. Ask questions like:

a. What is the setting of these verses?

b. Who are the main characters?

c. When and where is this taking place?

d. What is happening? Why?

DAY THREE

Read Daniel 6:1-15. Mark every reference to Daniel and add any new insights to your Daniel list in your notebook.

DAY FOUR

Read Daniel 6:16-24. Once again mark every reference to Daniel and add your insights to your list in your notebook.

DAY FIVE

Read through Daniel 6 again. This time, focus on the commissioners and satraps. Notice how they behave, what they do and why, and what their end is.

Think about what you observed. Do you see people do the same thing today? Does God?

DAY SIX

Read Daniel 6:25-28. Note the effect of Daniel's allegiance to his God. How did Darius feel about Daniel before this?

Think about Daniel 1. Daniel was about 15 years old in the first chapter of this book. About how old is he now? Has he changed or slackened in his commitment to his God? You may want to review your list of insights you are keeping on Daniel.

Write down any LFLs that you see in this chapter. Examine your commitment to the Lord over the years. Has your commitment grown stronger, or has it weakened? What do you think is the reason?

Record the theme of Daniel 6 on the DANIEL AT A GLANCE chart.

DAY SEVEN

Store in your heart: Daniel 6:26,27.

Read and discuss: Daniel 6:11-28; 2 Thessalonians 1:6-10.

QUESTIONS FOR DISCUSSION OR INDIVIDUAL STUDY

∾ What is the historical setting of this chapter? Who is reigning? What is his plan for governing Babylon?

∾ What is the main event of this chapter?

 a. Why does this happen to Daniel?

 b. What is the reason for the plot against Daniel?

 c. How do the men implement their plan?

 d. How does Daniel respond? Is his response true to his character?

 e. How does the king feel about Daniel's disobedience to his decree?

∾ How does God intervene in the situation?

 a. What happens to the men who plotted Daniel's death?

b. Do you think God was surprised at what happened to Daniel's enemies? Could God have stopped it?

c. According to 2 Thessalonians 1:6-10, how does what happened to Daniel fit with what God will do in the future?

❧ What do you learn about God from Daniel 6? What aspect of God's power is seen in this chapter that wasn't revealed in Daniel 1–5?

❧ As you review your list on Daniel this week, what do you learn about Daniel and his relationship to God?

a. Do you think it is possible to live an uncompromising lifestyle in today's society? Why or why not?

b. When you measure your life against Daniel's, how do you measure up?

THOUGHT FOR THE WEEK

Not only does God rule over the affairs of mankind, He is also able to close the mouths of lions! Since God does not change, since He is immutable, this truth still holds today! And since the truth of who He is holds, why do we fear the disapproval of man? The threats of man? The fear of man is a snare. You and I cannot be bond-servants of men. "For am I now seeking the favor of men, or of God? Or am I striving to please men? If I were still trying to please men, I would not be a bond-servant of Christ" (Galatians 1:10).

Like Daniel, Shadrach, Meshach, and Abed-nego, we must not compromise the Word of God or bend His commandments to save our lives. As His disciples, we must remember that he who would save his life will lose it, but that he who would lose his life for His sake and the gospel's will save it. We are only to fear God, who is able to cast both body and soul into hell.

O Beloved, may we not join the ranks of those who have compromised the Word of God in adverse circumstances. Let us join in heart with the martyrs of the faith who swore to be faithful unto death because our God is able to deliver us from the furnace of blazing fire—and from the lions' den. But even if He does not deliver us, may it be known that we will not serve nor worship any other god but our Most High God!

THE DETAILS OF THE LAST KINGDOM BEFORE THE SON OF MAN COMES

DAY ONE

Read Daniel 7. As you read, color, mark, or underline in a distinctive way every occurrence of the phrase, *I kept looking*.[5]

Now read Daniel 7:1-8 asking the 5 W's and an H. Note who is having the dream and visions, what the dream and visions are, when he is having them, and where this dream and the visions occur. Record your insights in your notebook.

Then consult the chart THE RULERS AND PROPHETS OF DANIEL'S TIME (page 19) and note the year these visions occur. Record this year in the margin of your Bible next to Daniel 7:1. At this point the book of Daniel ceases to be chronological.

Think about where this dream and the visions would fit chronologically into the first six chapters of Daniel.

DAY TWO

Read Daniel 7:1-12. One of the key words in this chapter is the word *beast(s)*. However, the emphasis is going to be on the *fourth beast;* therefore, mark every reference to the fourth beast so that it can be distinguished from the other beasts. You may want to simply underline the word *beast(s)* as well as any pronouns in a distinctive color and then color every reference to the *fourth beast* in an additional color. Make sure you mark every pronoun which refers to the fourth beast in the same way you mark *fourth beast.* Note the number of the beasts mentioned.

Read Daniel 2:36-45 again. Are there any parallels between these two sections?

~~~~

DAY THREE

</center>

Read Daniel 7:1-16. Mark every reference to the word *horn(s).* You'll see that just as the fourth beast is singled out from the others, so *another horn* is singled out for attention from the ten. Mark this other horn in a distinctive way so that you can easily distinguish it from the ten. Also mark any pronouns which refer to this horn in the same way. See who *the Ancient of Days* is and mark every reference and pronoun to Him in the same way you have other references to Him. Finally, mark every reference to the *Son of Man* along with any pronouns which refer to Him.

When you finish, either make a new list in your notebook or add to your current lists everything you learn from marking these key words. Leave room to continue your list on the little horn that comes up among the ten horns. If you are making notes on things you learn about God in your Bible, don't forget to continue that.

DAY FOUR

Read Daniel 7:17-28 and mark the key words you marked in Daniel 7:1-16. Don't forget to mark their pronouns in the same way. Also watch for any reference to *the Ancient of Days* and the synonyms, *the Highest One*[6] and *the Most High*. Mark these phrases and pronouns all in the same way.

Add to your lists in your notebook everything you learn from this passage about the little horn, the Ancient of Days, and the fourth beast.

For quick reference, next to Daniel 7:17 you might want to write the word "Interpretation" in the margin. Then, next to Daniel 7:2, write the word "Vision."

DAY FIVE

Read Daniel 7:17-28 again. This time mark every reference to the *saints* and their pronouns in another distinctive way.* Also mark every reference to time. In biblical reckoning, the phrase "time, times, and half a time"[7] is 3½ years; therefore, mark this phrase as one time reference.

In your notebook list everything you learn from marking the word *saints*.

Also add to your list anything else you may have seen in Daniel 7:17-28 about the other horn.

---

* Remember, Daniel is an Old Testament book and its prophecies relate to the nation of Israel. The church was a mystery hidden until the time of Paul. The mystery of the church is that it is comprised of Jew and Gentile in one body (Ephesians 2,3). Romans 11:25-29 teaches us that God is not finished with the nation of Israel because the gifts and calling of God stand firm. (See also Jeremiah 31:35-37.) Someday all of Israel existing at the time that the Deliverer comes from Zion will be saved. I believe these are the saints of the Highest One. Therefore, I mark the references to the saints in Daniel with a blue star of David like this ✡ .

DAY SIX

Record the theme of Daniel 7 on the DANIEL AT A GLANCE chart. Also record any LFLs that you find in this chapter.

Now, beloved student, put on your thinking cap and let's reason together from the Scriptures. If, as Hebrews 5:14 teaches, you "train your senses" and chew on this strong meat of the Word, you'll amaze yourself at what you are able to understand on your own from observing the text (see Hebrews 5:14). So get the facts down and then think about all you have seen by carefully observing the Word of God.

Using Daniel 2:36-45, fill in the details on the sketch on the next page where the gold, silver, etc., go. Then, using the chart WORLD KINGDOMS FROM DANIEL'S TIME ON (page 33), write beside the sketch which kingdoms the gold, silver, etc., represent. Keep in mind that kings and kingdoms refer to the same thing since the king rules over the kingdom.

On the chart on the following page, where would you place:

a. the four beasts of Daniel 7? (Write down what each beast is like, i.e., lion, bear.)

b. the ten horns?

c. the little horn?

d. the Son of Man given dominion, glory, and a kingdom that is everlasting?

e. the saints taking possession of the kingdom?

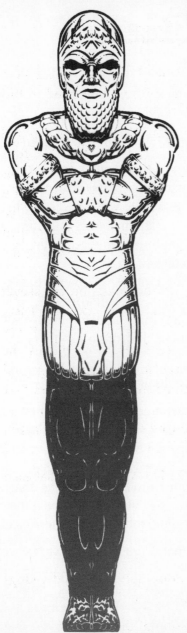

THE STATUE OF
DANIEL 2

THE BEASTS AND
LITTLE HORN OF
DANIEL 7

DAY SEVEN

 Store in your heart: Daniel 7:17,18 or Daniel 7:23-25.

Read and discuss: Daniel 7:17-28.

QUESTIONS FOR DISCUSSION OR INDIVIDUAL STUDY

Sharing any interpretation of this chapter before thoroughly observing and recording observations of the text could create great confusion. Be sure to review exactly what the text says and finish the questions—then you have a plumb line by which to determine the accuracy (the straightness) of each interpretation.

Remember and remind the group that this is a *survey course* of Daniel. Carefully doing the homework will build a solid foundation for further study and for examining what they are taught on the book and/or on prophecy at a later time.

∞ Describe what Daniel 7 is about.

∞ Where does Daniel 7 fit chronologically into the first six chapters of Daniel? How do you know? If you have a drawing board, draw a diagram of the statue in Daniel 2 and see what information the members of the class can fill in from memory. If they can't complete the chart, have them look at the work they've done to refresh their memories. Be sure to place the following on the sketch:

a. the four beasts of Daniel 7 (write down what each beast is like)

b. the ten horns

c. the little horn

   d. the Son of Man given dominion, glory, and a kingdom that is everlasting

   e. the saints taking possession of the kingdom

∾ Explain why each is placed where it is.

∾ What do you learn from Daniel 7 about the little horn that comes up from among the ten? Make a list on the board of what the class shares, making sure the following is covered. Be sure the answers are from the text!

   a. Where does the little horn come from, and how is it described?

   b. What will the little horn do to some of the other horns?

   c. How long will the saints be overpowered by the little horn?

   d. What will bring the little horn's rule to an end?

   e. What will happen to the little horn?

   f. What will follow this event?

∾ Discuss what you learn about the following from Daniel 7:

   a. the three beasts and their fate

   b. the saints

   c. the Son of Man

   d. the Ancient of Days

∾ In the additional light of Daniel 7, who or what does the stone in Daniel 2 represent? Why?

∾ If you haven't covered it yet, ask, "What did you observe by marking the various references to time? When does the 'time, times, and half a time' occur? What brings it to an end?"

∾ Talk about God's blueprint for prophecy in these two chapters. Discuss the extent of the time span from the Babylonian kingdom to the coming of the Son of Man and the setting up of His kingdom. Although we may not understand everything about the four kingdoms (the four beasts) and where that fourth one (Roman Empire) has gone, think about what we do know from Daniel's blueprint of prophecy!

Remember, a blueprint gives you an overall plan. The book of Daniel is the blueprint for prophecy, giving you the overall picture of events from Babylon to the setting up of God's kingdom on earth. However, there are more detailed diagrams for various parts of the whole. Other portions in the Word of God give additional details of what is going to take place—but Daniel gives the blueprint!

THOUGHT FOR THE WEEK

God tells us that He declares the end from the beginning. In Amos 3:7 we read, "Surely the Lord GOD does nothing unless He reveals His secret counsel to His servants the prophets." What the prophets wrote was not of their own devising, rather, as 2 Peter 1:20,21 says, they spoke as they were moved by the Spirit of God.

What you are studying, Beloved, is a sure word of prophecy to which you do well to take heed and live accordingly (2 Peter 1:19).

If you let Scripture say what it says without adding your own interpretation or squeezing it into your own mold of systematic theology, then the Stone is coming to crush the feet of the statue when its feet are iron mingled with clay and has ten toes (kings). It is in those days that the God of heaven will set up His kingdom which will endure forever. Daniel 7:13 shows that it's the Son of Man who is given "a kingdom, that all the peoples, nations, and *men of every* language might serve Him. His dominion is an everlasting dominion which will not pass away; and His kingdom is one which will not be destroyed" (Daniel 7:14).

It must be a visible kingdom, for the time will arrive when the saints take possession of it (Daniel 7:22).

> Then the sovereignty, the dominion, and the greatness of *all* the kingdoms under the whole heaven will be given to the people of the saints of the Highest One; His kingdom *will* be an everlasting kingdom, and all the dominions will serve and obey Him (Daniel 7:27).

This is God's blueprint for prophecy—and every other prophecy fits somewhere in this broad picture and time frame.

THE RAM, THE GOAT, AND ISRAEL

DAY ONE

Read Daniel 8. As you read, note when this vision takes place and how it relates chronologically to the vision of Daniel 7. Record your insights in your notebook; also record any insights you glean about Daniel on your Daniel list.

DAY TWO

Read Daniel 8:1-14 and mark every reference to the *ram* and the *goat*. Be sure you mark each distinctly from the other and mark each word's pronouns accordingly. Also mark the references to the *rather small horn* (and its pronouns) that comes out of one of the four horns of the goat.

Be very accurate in your observations related to the various horns mentioned in this chapter, or you'll handle the text incorrectly—especially after observing the little horn in Daniel 7. Let the text speak for itself (you'll be able to do that through careful observation).

DAY THREE

Read Daniel 8:1-14 again. Mark every reference to time.

Look at the map below and identify where Daniel is in the vision.

Now examine Daniel 8:1-14 in the light of the 5 W's and an H. Note who is having the vision, when he has it, where he is, what he sees, who the main characters are, etc. Record your insights in your notebook.

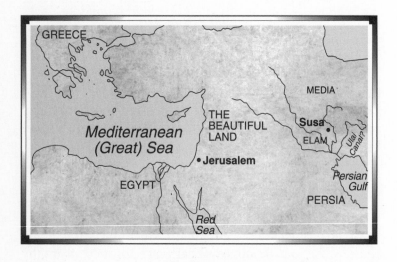

DAY FOUR

Read Daniel 8:15-27. Continue to mark the key words you marked on Day Two.

In the margin of your Bible, next to Daniel 8:15, you might want to write "Interpretation" and next to Daniel 8:3 write "Vision" for quick reference.

DAY FIVE

Read Daniel 8:15-27 again. This time mark all references to time and mark the phrase *time of the end*[8] in a distinctive way from the other time phrases. Although it is a time phrase, it needs its own distinctive mark. If you think the phrase *the final period of the indignation*[9] is in the same time period denoted by the phrase *time of the end,* then mark it in the same way. Also, note "who" the horns belong to in Daniel 8.

List in your notebook everything you learn from Daniel 8 about the ram and the goat.

Take what you learned from Daniel 2 and 7 and transfer it to the copy of the sketch of the statue on page 66. Now add what you observe from Daniel 8. (Noting again what you see is a learning exercise and will help you remember the content of these chapters.)

Daniel 2 is the main blueprint; Daniel 7 gives the big picture in another form (that of the beasts) but fills in more details about the fourth kingdom (beast). Then Daniel 8 focuses on the details of two of the kingdoms of Daniel 2, which are also represented in Daniel 7 by two beasts. However, in Daniel 8 we see different animals than before. These animals will illustrate certain details about these two kingdoms.*

Therefore, when you add the ram and the goat of Daniel 8, put them opposite the two beasts you think they represent in Daniel 7, which are the two kingdoms of Daniel 2.

---

* A very helpful and interesting book to have in your library is *Josephus: The Essential Writings* (Kregel). It is enlightening to read the account of the Medo-Persian and Greek kingdoms and how they interfaced with the nation of Israel.

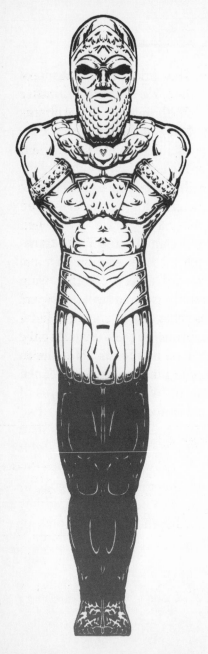

DANIEL 2　　DANIEL 7　　DANIEL 8

DAY SIX

Read Daniel 8:15-27 one final time. This time mark every reference to the king who will arise in the latter period, and then in your notebook make a list of everything you learn from the text about this king.

Watch the time phrases you marked. If any of them pertain to this king, write that on your list.

Note when Daniel had the vision of Daniel 8, what kingdom is in power at the time, and the instructions given Daniel in 8:26. Then ask, "What kingdom is in power when Daniel's ministry ends?" Look at the charts THE RULERS AND PROPHETS OF DANIEL'S TIME (page 19) and WORLD KINGDOMS FROM DANIEL'S TIME ON (page 33). How long after Daniel's ministry does Greece come to power? Alexander the Great was the one who conquered the Medes and the Persians, but at the age of 33 he died suddenly. Since there was no appointed heir, four of his generals eventually divided his kingdom into four regions (see the chart below).

The Division of Alexander the Great's Empire			
Lysimachus took Thrace and Bithynia	**Cassander** took Macedonia	**Ptolemy I Soter** took Egypt	**Seleucus I Nicator** took Syria

Ptolemy I Soter and Seleucus I Nicator began a succession of competing dynasties for which the land of Israel became a pawn.

Record the theme of Daniel 8 on the DANIEL AT A GLANCE chart.

DAY SEVEN

Store in your heart: Daniel 8:20,21. These verses will help you remember the essence of this chapter.

Read and discuss: Daniel 8:15-27.

QUESTIONS FOR DISCUSSION OR INDIVIDUAL STUDY

∾ What two kingdoms does Daniel 8 focus on?

∾ What do you observe about the ram in Daniel 8?

∾ What do you observe about the goat in Daniel 8?

∾ Where do the ram and the goat fit in relation to the dreams of Daniel 2 and 7? Have a student draw a sketch of the statue and fill in the kingdoms of Daniel 2. Then have another student show how Daniel 7 relates to Daniel 2. Have a third student show where Daniel 8 fits into the scheme of things. Have the group discuss why the students placed things where they did.

∾ What did you learn about the "rather small horn" that comes from one of the four horns of the goat? Review everything you observed from the text.

∾ What do you learn about the king who will arise as mentioned in Daniel 8:23? List your insights about this king on the board and then ask, "Do you see any relationship between the 'rather small horn' and the king?" Make sure they explain their answers from the text.

∾ What do you learn from marking the time phrases, including *the final period of the indignation*[10] and *time of the end*[11]?

∾ When Daniel has the vision recorded in chapter 8, what kingdom is in power at the time he is given the instructions in 8:26?

a. What kingdom is in power when Daniel dies?

b. How does this fit with the history you read on Day Six?

c. What do you see about the awesomeness of Daniel's prophecies?

THOUGHT FOR THE WEEK

God told Daniel what was going to transpire in regard to the Medo-Persian Empire and the Grecian Empire when neither was a major world power. In the days when the Babylonians still ruled, God gave Daniel a vision—a sure word of prophecy that would explain the future to the nation of Israel. Because of the detailed historical accuracy of the book of Daniel, some theologians say this book had to be written after the fact and not before and therefore Daniel did not write the book of Daniel! But is this true? All we have to go on is the Word of God and what we observe from the text, or we can listen to the word of man and what comes from his mouth and what is written in his commentaries!

Whom will you listen to? Whom will you believe, child of God? Man, who is limited by his understanding, his education—or the Word of God given to us by an infinite God who cannot lie and knows the beginning from the end? Will you believe the God who rules over history—"The LORD of hosts" who "has sworn saying, 'Surely, just as I have intended so it has happened, and just as I have planned so it will stand'" (Isaiah 14:24)?

God tells us, "For the LORD of hosts has planned, and who can frustrate it? And as for His stretched-out hand, who can turn it back?" (Isaiah 14:27).

Daniel had a vision that came from God—a vision that pertained to many days in the future. You can believe it, Beloved—believe the *whole* book of Daniel. It is the sure Word of God, a light that shines in a dark place. Listen to God and believe what man says only if it lines up with the Word of God.

KEEP YOUR EYES ON ISRAEL— GOD'S TIME CLOCK

∾∾∾∾

DAY ONE

Read Daniel 9 for an overview. As you read, mark every reference to time. Also mark references to Daniel and add new insights to your list in your notebook.

Daniel 9:1-3 gives you the historical setting of this chapter. You also see in these verses why Daniel is moved to pray and fast. Refer to THE RULERS AND PROPHETS OF DANIEL'S TIME (page 19) and note what year Daniel 9 occurs. Next to Daniel 9:1,2 in your Bible note this year. Then find the chapter in the first six chapters that parallels this time.

DAY TWO

Read Daniel 9:1-3. Next to Daniel 9:2 in your Bible, write the cross-reference Jeremiah 29:1-14, and then read this passage. Reading this passage is what caused Daniel to seek the Lord in prayer and fasting.

Why would the Jews be in captivity for 70 years? Why not more or less? Read 2 Chronicles 36:20-23. Give special attention to verse 21 and what it says about the land enjoying its sabbaths. Then read Leviticus 25:1-7 and 26:27-35. During a time span of 490 years the children of Israel had not given the land its sabbath rest, therefore they owed God 70 sabbaths—70 years.

By the first year of Darius, how many of the 70 years of captivity had passed?

DAY THREE

Read Daniel 9:1-19 and mark the phrase *we have sinned.* In another distinctive way mark *Jerusalem* and phrases referring to it (for example, *Your city,*[12] *Your holy mountain,*[13] etc.).

Also watch for and mark how often Daniel cries out to God: *O Lord, our God, O my God,* etc. When you finish, list in your notebook what you learn about Daniel's people and what you learn about God from this portion of Scripture.

DAY FOUR

Read Daniel 9:20-27. Mark the word *sin*[14] in the same way you marked *we have sinned.* Also mark *Jerusalem* and phrases referring to it (*the holy mountain of my God,*[15] *holy city,* etc.) as you did in Day Three.

Read Daniel 9:24-27 and examine this prophecy given to Daniel in light of the 5 W's and an H. Who is speaking? To whom? About what? What has to happen within the seventy weeks? What is the order of events?

Record your insights in your notebook.

DAY FIVE

In Daniel 9:24 the word for *weeks* is literally "sevens,"[16] therefore it is 70 sevens or 490. The question, then, would be, "Is it referring to 490 hours, days, weeks, or years?" Since none of the others fit the time frame, I believe it is a reference to 490 years. However, you need to see this for yourself. So, as we carefully move through the text and compare Scripture with Scripture, hangeth thou in there. In order to be sure we are considering the same translation, the text printed out below is from the NAS.

> 24 Seventy weeks have been decreed for your people and your holy city, to finish the transgression, to make an end of sin, to make atonement for iniquity, to bring in everlasting righteousness, to seal up vision and prophecy and to anoint the most holy place.

> 25 So you are to know and discern that from the issuing of a decree to restore and rebuild Jerusalem until Messiah the Prince there will be seven weeks and sixty-two weeks; it will be built again, with plaza and moat, even in times of distress.

> 26 Then after the sixty-two weeks the Messiah will be cut off and have nothing, and the people of the prince who is to come will destroy the city and the sanctuary. And its end will come with a flood; even to the end there will be war; desolations are determined.

27 And he will make a firm covenant with the many for one week, but in the middle of the week he will put a stop to sacrifice and grain offering; and on the wing of abominations *will come* one who makes desolate, even until a complete destruction, one that is decreed, is poured out on the one who makes desolate.

Read Daniel 9:24. Note for whom and what city this prophecy has been decreed and record your insights on the chart THE SEVENTY WEEKS OF DANIEL (page 75).

Also list everything that must transpire in these 70 sevens or 490 years.

If you want to note these insights in your Bible, you could write it in the margin or simply number each event in the text itself (over every "to…"). For example, you would put:

1
"to finish the transgression"

2
"to make an end of sin"

3
"to…"

Now read Daniel 9:25 and mark *from* and *until*[17] and note what happens in this time frame. Also note the length of time. Add 7 and 62 and what do you get? How many "weeks" or "sevens" are yet to be accounted for (fulfilled)?

In Daniel 9:26, note what happens after the 69 weeks but is not included in the actual 70-week period. Note who it is that destroys the city (Jerusalem) and the sanctuary (the temple built by Herod). Record this information on THE SEVENTY WEEKS OF DANIEL chart (page 75).

The Seventy Weeks of Daniel

This prophecy is decreed for:

What must transpire in these seventy weeks:

1.

2.

3.

4.

5.

6.

City and sanctuary destroyed by:

Events of the last week:

1.

2.

3.

How the week is divided: Length of each division:

In Daniel 9:27 one more week, the final week of the 70, is mentioned. Record what happens in this last week on the chart THE SEVENTY WEEKS OF DANIEL. Note how the week is divided and the resulting length of each division.

Who does the "he" in this verse refer to? Go back to verse 26 and mark the word *Messiah*[18] and the phrase *the prince who is to come*[19] distinctively from one another. "He" refers to one of these—but there is debate over who "he" refers to. From simply observing the text, to which does "he" refer? Make sure you see what "he" does at the beginning of the week and in the middle of the week. And don't miss what happens to the one who makes desolate!

DAY SIX

Read Daniel 9:24-27 again. Review what you observed yesterday and what you noted on the chart THE SEVENTY WEEKS OF DANIEL (page 75). Note on the chart the Scripture from Daniel 9:24-27 that describes each event. For instance, at the beginning of the chart where you wrote, "A decree to restore and rebuild Jerusalem," note "9:25." Put 9:26 and 9:27 where they fit on the chart.

Now, look up the following cross-references. Watch for any references to time. You may want to note these cross-references on THE SEVENTY WEEKS OF DANIEL chart. (If you don't have time to look up all the cross-references, do what you can now and come back to them later.)

Compare Daniel 9:24 with Nehemiah 1:1–2:8.

Compare Daniel 9:26 with:

a. Matthew 27:33-37,45-53—Messiah cut off. Jesus died sometime around A.D. 29.

b. Luke 19:37-44; 21:20-24—The people (of "the prince who is to come") will destroy the city and the sanctuary. History tells us that Jerusalem and the temple were destroyed in A.D. 70 by Titus, a Roman general.

Compare Daniel 9:27 with Daniel 7:24-26; Matthew 24:15-21; 2 Thessalonians 2:3,4,8; Revelation 13:3-8; 19:11-16, 19,20. Write any new insights from these cross-references in your notebook.

Add your insights to your list on Daniel and God.

Do you see any LFLs in this chapter? If so, note these in your notebook.

Record the theme of Daniel 9 on the DANIEL AT A GLANCE chart.

DAY SEVEN

 Store in your heart: Daniel 9:24-27.
Read and discuss: Daniel 9:24-27.

QUESTIONS FOR DISCUSSION OR INDIVIDUAL STUDY

∞ What is the historical setting of Daniel 9?

a. When do these events occur?

b. How far away is Daniel from the end of the 70 years of captivity?

∞ Why does Judah go into captivity for the specific period of 70 years? (This captivity is dated from the first siege of Jerusalem in 605 B.C. when Daniel was taken captive.)

a. What was the sabbath rest of the land?

b. What is God's warning in Leviticus 26:27-35?

∽ For whom and what city was the prophecy of Daniel 9:24-27 decreed?

∽ What six things have to transpire during the 70 weeks? List these and go through them one by one. Check off any that have been completed. Have they all come to pass in regard to the nation of Israel?

∽ How would you explain the events described in Daniel 9:24-27?

∽ As you do the following, use only the text.

a. Draw a time line on the board as you go through Daniel 9:24-27, showing the weeks and the relationship of the events to the weeks.

b. Note carefully what happens between week 69 and week 70.

c. Does the text tell you how long the gap of time is between weeks 69 and 70?

d. Has there been a *literal historical fulfillment* of the first 69 weeks in respect to the Jews and Jerusalem? The events that occur after the 69th week? The events described in the 70th week? What does this tell you about the 70th week?

e. Discuss the cross-references you looked up on Day Six for Daniel 9:27; Daniel 7:24-26; Matthew 24:15-21; 2 Thessalonians 2:3,4,8; Revelation 13:3-8; 19:11-16,19,20. As you discuss these, note any references to time and how this compares with Daniel 9:27 and the final week or seven years. Since this is not an in-depth study on Daniel, you may not have all the answers. This question may raise more questions. However, simply look at what was observed in the text and discuss your insights. Don't get into speculation—that is not the purpose of this *survey* of the book of Daniel.*

∾ What do you learn from Daniel's prayer?

a. How does it speak to your heart?

b. Is it a relevant prayer for today?

c. When was the last time you sought God in genuine humility with prayer and fasting? What do you think would happen if God's people did more praying and fasting?

d. What prompted Daniel to fast and pray? What was he reading? What do you think would happen if there were more people like Daniel—people of the Word of God?

THOUGHT FOR THE WEEK

Israel is God's time clock. If you want to know what is going on in the world today, observe carefully what is happening in Israel. Not one word of God will fail in regard to Israel. Romans 11:25-29 tells us that when the fullness of the Gentiles has come, then "all Israel will be saved; just as it is written, 'THE DELIVERER WILL COME FROM ZION, HE WILL REMOVE UNGODLINESS FROM JACOB [Israel]. THIS IS MY

---

* If you would like to do a more in-depth study on the book of Daniel, our Precept Upon Precept Bible Study course on Daniel will take you deeper into the Word of God. For more information, call Precept Ministries International at 800-763-8280, visit our website at www.precept.org, or fill out and mail the response card at the back of this book.

COVENANT WITH THEM, WHEN I TAKE AWAY THEIR SINS.'"
Daniel 9:24 gives us a clear prophecy regarding the Jews
and their holy city, Jerusalem, and the seventy weeks of
time in which the transgression will be finished—the end
of sin, an atonement for iniquity made, everlasting righ-
teousness brought in, the vision and prophecy sealed up,
and the most holy place anointed.

All those things have not yet been fulfilled in respect to
Israel, but because the gifts and calling of God are irrevo-
cable, they will be (Romans 11:29). If you take God literally, in the single sense in which He speaks in His Word, you
will realize that Israel will never cease being a nation. God
watches over His Word to perform it. And because His
promises for Israel will not fail, neither will His promises to
you. You can rest on it—it's called the rest of faith.

HEAVENLY RULERS OVER EARTHLY KINGDOMS

DAY ONE

Read Daniel 10. List in your notebook everything you learn about Daniel from this chapter. Our emphasis this first time through the chapter is to focus on Daniel as a person and on his relationship to God. Tomorrow we will look specifically at the vision, so don't focus on that today. Be sure to note how Daniel is referred to in verses 11 and 19 and mark the phrase used to refer to him in a distinctive way.

Don't forget to add to your list on Daniel and to note any LFLs you see.

DAY TWO

Read through Daniel 10 again and mark the word *vision* in a distinctive way. As you read, note what Daniel is telling the reader about. Where is he when it happens? When does it happen? Exactly what happens? (You may have observed this yesterday, but make sure you didn't miss anything.)

Look at the relationship of verse 1 to the rest of the chapter. Note what this verse tells you about the "message." Record all your insights in your notebook.

DAY THREE

Read Daniel 10 again. Note who is speaking to Daniel by marking every reference to this person. Also mark every reference to *Michael.*

Make a list in your notebook of everything you learn about the person sent to give Daniel understanding. Make sure you note what this person was sent to do because this is key to the remainder of the book of Daniel. Also make a list of all you learn about Michael.

Be certain you observe exactly who this vision pertains to. This observation is critical. (If you think there are *two* persons communicating with Daniel in this chapter, note who you think they are and your reasoning.)

DAY FOUR

Now read Daniel 10:14–11:4 as if there were no chapter break. Watch carefully who is speaking (especially in 11:1), the time he is speaking of, and who he wants to be an encouragement to and a protection for.

What did you see? Did you notice that Daniel 11 is a continuation of what began in Daniel 10—part of the same revelation? If not, read it again. I want to make sure that you observe the text carefully and that you realize that Daniel 11:1 doesn't begin a whole new prophecy given at a different time.

DAY FIVE

Read Daniel 10:14–12:13 marking every reference to time. Also mark any reference to *Michael*. Note the names of specific kingdoms that are referred to. Don't try to figure out what everything means because that will come later!

Our last three weeks of study will be devoted to studying these awesomely accurate chapters. In your notebook, record what kingdom the vision begins with and what events chapter 12 of Daniel ends with. This will give you a sense of the years spanned in Daniel's final vision.

DAY SIX

Yesterday you saw two specific kingdoms mentioned by name: Persia and Greece.

Go back and read Daniel 8:15-22 again. Do you see any correlation between these verses in Daniel 8 and what you read in Daniel 10:20–11:4? If so, note the parallels in your notebook.

Record the theme of Daniel 10 on the DANIEL AT A GLANCE chart.

DAY SEVEN

Store in your heart: Daniel 10:11,14. (If two verses are too much, memorize verse 14.)
Read and discuss: Daniel 10:1–11:4.

QUESTIONS FOR DISCUSSION OR INDIVIDUAL STUDY

∿ What is the setting of Daniel 10?

    a. Where is Daniel?

    b. What happens?

    c. When does it happen?

∿ What do you learn about Daniel from this chapter?

    a. How is he referred to?

    b. What do you learn about his relationship to God?

    c. How does what he has seen and heard affect him?

∿ What do you learn from this chapter about the person who relates this vision to Daniel?

    a. Do you think one person or two persons came to Daniel in this chapter? Why?

    b. What kind of a conflict does this person encounter?

    c. What is the result of the conflict?

    d. Who is the conflict with and who comes to his aid?

    e. What did this person come to do in respect to Daniel?

    f. Is there any relationship between this person and the "I" of Daniel 11:1,2? How do you know?

∿ What do you learn from Daniel 10:1–11:4 about the vision?

    a. What does this vision concern?

    b. To whom does the vision pertain?

    c. How certain is this vision? How do you know?

    d. When does the vision come to a close? With what event? Where in Daniel is this explained?

∾ What do you learn about the kingdoms of Persia and Greece?

    a. Where are these kingdoms mentioned in Daniel 10 and 11?

    b. How does what Daniel 10 and 11 say about Persia and Greece compare with Daniel 8?

∾ Why do you think Daniel was referred to as a "man of high esteem"?

∾ How do you want to be known before God and His angelic host? What do you think it will take? Are you willing? Why?

THOUGHT FOR THE WEEK

The book of Daniel seems to give us a glimpse into the authorities, dominions, and rulers "in heavenly places." When you compare what Daniel 10 says about the conflict with "the prince of the kingdom of Persia" with other passages of Scripture, it seems that, just as there are kings and rulers over earthly kingdoms, there are spiritual rulers in heavenly places that influence earthly kingdoms. Behind the earthly conflicts are heavenly conflicts.

When tempting Jesus, Satan said he would give Him all the kingdoms of this world if He would fall down and worship him. Jesus did not argue that the kingdoms of the world were not Satan's to give because, for now, Satan is the prince of this world, the prince of the power of the air.

When Satan deceived Eve and led Adam and Eve into sin, Adam lost his God-given leadership over the earth. That is why, at this present time, Satan has the kingdoms to give: "The whole world lies in *the power of* the evil one" (1 John 5:19)!

If you study world history, it is obvious that from the beginning of the nations after the flood, from the time of the tower of Babel, man has been in rebellion against God. How well Psalm 2:1-3 describes this rebellion: "Why are the nations in an uproar, and the peoples devising a vain thing? The kings of the earth take their stand, and the rulers take counsel together against the LORD and against His Anointed, saying, 'Let us tear their fetters apart, and cast away their cords from us!'"

The one with the human appearance who appeared to Daniel gave him a vision that spanned the time of the Persian rule over the nation of Israel to the final days when the regular sacrifice is abolished and the abomination of desolation is set up. The final days, as explained in several passages in Daniel, is when the prince who is to come, the little horn of Daniel, will set up the abomination of desolation and then come into direct conflict with the nation of Israel for a time, times, and half a time, until the power of the holy people is shattered. That's 3½ years of unimaginable agony for the nation of Israel and the Jews scattered around the world. Then the stone will crush the feet of the statue, topple all nations to the ground, and the Lord God will set up His kingdom which will never be destroyed.

Until that time, however, there will be conflict between the nations and Israel, between the children of the devil and the children of God, between Satan and his fallen heavenly host and God and His angelic host. That conflict will not only be between mere flesh and blood but also "against the rulers, against the powers, against the world forces of this darkness, against the spiritual forces of wickedness in the heavenly places" (Ephesians 6:12).

Several Old Testament passages give us insight into the connection between earthly kings and the "spiritual" rulers connected with them. For instance, just as there was an earthly leader of Tyre, so Ezekiel 28 tells us of a "king"— the king behind the leader, the king who was an anointed cherub and was cast out from the mountain of God.

Isaiah 14 tells us of the king of Babylon whom he describes as the one fallen from heaven, the star of the morning, the one who wanted to ascend above the stars of God and make himself like the Most High. Yet God would thrust him—the one who shook kingdoms—down to Sheol to the recesses of the pit.

Yet truly, "He who sits in the heavens laughs, the Lord scoffs at them. Then He will speak to them in His anger and terrify them in His fury." Why? Because God says, "As for Me, I have installed My King upon Zion, My holy mountain." Thus the Ancient of Days says to the Son of Man, His Son, "Ask of Me, and I will surely give the nations as Your inheritance, and the very ends of the earth as Your possession. You shalt break them with a rod of iron, You shall shatter them like earthenware" (Psalm 2:4-6,8,9).

Daniel, the man of high esteem, was on the winning side. No one will defeat God or alter His purposes and plan for His covenant people, Israel, the apple (pupil) of His eye. Someday Daniel will rise again for his allotted portion at the end of the age.

O Beloved, there is a heavenly conflict. Yes, there is a devil and, yes, he does have a demonic host to do his bidding. But there is also God. He is the Most High God and He does according to His will in the armies of heaven and among the inhabitants of the earth. No one can stay His hands...and no one can say to Him, "What doest Thou?" God knows what He is doing and He is going to bring these events to pass. Then He is going to install His King. And we, as children of God, will be there for His coronation!

So stand firm. Don't waver. Be a person of high esteem in the eyes of God. Follow Daniel's example as you live in the midst of a crooked and perverse generation. Hold forth God's light with your life, with your lips. Maranatha! Come, Lord Jesus!

God's Blueprint for the Intertestament Period

As you get ready to do this week's lesson, I want to encourage you to persevere. Daniel 11 is not an easy chapter to study, but you don't want to miss it because it lays the groundwork for Daniel 12, which is so critical to the future. If you are going to have a good understanding of prophecy, you need to understand God's blueprint that He has given in this awesome book. So hangeth thou in there, Beloved. Be a good soldier of Christ Jesus. Watch your time this week and do what is necessary to have time for your studies. You are almost to the finish line, and only those who finish qualify for the prize.

This week is going to be heavy on history. And even though history may not be your favorite subject, it is very significant to the Word of God. As I mentioned earlier, history is "His story," so read it carefully!

DAY ONE

Read Daniel 11. As you read, remember Daniel 10–12 covers one vision. Also remember that the chapter divisions are man-made. Mark or underline references to the *king of the South* and the *king of the North*. Mark each king in different ways. Also mark any pronouns which refer to each king. Mark these very carefully, being certain you know which king is being referred to.

DAY TWO

Apart from the hindsight of history, Daniel 11 is difficult to understand. Yet, it is also a masterpiece of prophecy. Let's deal with the chapter segment by segment.

In the first four verses of Daniel 11, two kingdoms are mentioned by name. In your notebook under two columns, Persia and Greece, list what you learn about these two kingdoms from observing the text.

Look at the chart THE RULERS AND PROPHETS OF DANIEL'S TIME (page 19). According to this chart, what were the names of the three kings who reigned after Darius the Mede? (Do not consider Smerdis in your observation since he reigned only a very short time—possibly only days—before he was killed by his brother.) The fourth Persian king in Daniel 11:2, Artaxerxes I (Ahasuerus, also called Xerxes), is the Persian king mentioned in Nehemiah 1,2.

In your notebook make a chart using the following headings for four columns: Daniel 2:39; Daniel 7:6; Daniel 8:21,22; and Daniel 11:3,4. Then read each reference and write your observations in the appropriate column. Note that in Daniel 2 and 7 the third kingdom is described. Record who the mighty king of Daniel 11:3,4 is.

On the chart on the next page, find the king of Daniel 11:3,4. How does Daniel 11:3,4 relate to the symbolism of the "four" wings, heads, and horns in Daniel 7 and 8?

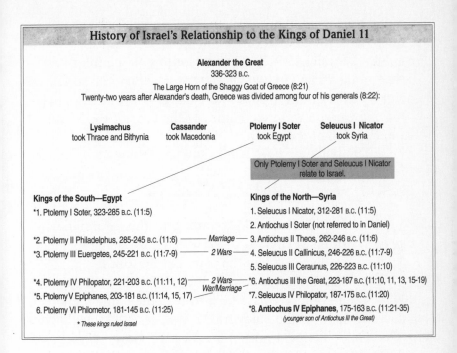

History of Israel's Relationship to the Kings of Daniel 11

Alexander the Great
336-323 B.C.

The Large Horn of the Shaggy Goat of Greece (8:21)
Twenty-two years after Alexander's death, Greece was divided among four of his generals (8:22):

Lysimachus	**Cassander**	**Ptolemy I Soter**	**Seleucus I Nicator**
took Thrace and Bithynia	took Macedonia	took Egypt	took Syria

Only Ptolemy I Soter and Seleucus I Nicator relate to Israel.

Kings of the South—Egypt

*1. Ptolemy I Soter, 323-285 B.C. (11:5)

*2. Ptolemy II Philadelphus, 285-245 B.C. (11:6) —————— Marriage ——

*3. Ptolemy III Euergetes, 245-221 B.C. (11:7-9) —————— 2 Wars ——

*4. Ptolemy IV Philopator, 221-203 B.C. (11:11, 12) —— 2 Wars ——
                                                    War/Marriage
*5. Ptolemy V Epiphanes, 203-181 B.C. (11:14, 15, 17) ——

6. Ptolemy VI Philometor, 181-145 B.C. (11:25)

* These kings ruled Israel

Kings of the North—Syria

1. Seleucus I Nicator, 312-281 B.C. (11:5)

2. Antiochus I Soter (not referred to in Daniel)

3. Antiochus II Theos, 262-246 B.C. (11:6)

4. Seleucus II Callinicus, 246-226 B.C. (11:7-9)

5. Seleucus III Ceraunus, 226-223 B.C. (11:10)

*6. Antiochus III the Great, 223-187 B.C. (11:10, 11, 13, 15-19)

*7. Seleucus IV Philopator, 187-175 B.C. (11:20)

*8. **Antiochus IV Epiphanes**, 175-163 B.C. (11:21-35)
(younger son of Antiochus III the Great)

DAY THREE

When Alexander the Great of Greece died, his kingdom eventually was divided between four of his generals: Lysimachus, Cassander, Ptolemy I Soter, and Seleucus I Nicator. That's the significance of the "four" wings, heads, and horns in these prophetic descriptions!

The book of Daniel is concerned with the last two of these generals because they, along with their descendants, ruled over Israel at various times.

Look again at the chart HISTORY OF ISRAEL'S RELATIONSHIP TO THE KINGS OF DANIEL 11 to gain an understanding of the conflict between the king of the South and the king of the North and to note the names of particular kings and the time in which each ruled.

Read Daniel 11:5-20. Then, according to the information on the chart HISTORY OF ISRAEL'S RELATIONSHIP TO THE KINGS OF DANIEL 11, record in the margin of your Bible by the appropriate verse the names of the king of the South and the king of the North.

DAY FOUR

Read Daniel 11:21-35. According to the information given on the chart HISTORY OF ISRAEL'S RELATIONSHIP TO THE KINGS OF DANIEL 11, fill in the names of the kings.

Now read MAJOR EVENTS IN ISRAEL'S HISTORY on pages 111–24.* If you don't have time to read the entire section included here in the study guide now, read the portion, "The Greek Period Under Alexander the Great," through the first two paragraphs of "The Maccabean Period."

DAY FIVE

Daniel 11:21-35 gives a lengthy description of Antiochus IV Epiphanes. Reread this passage carefully and mark the following words or phrases, each in a distinctive way: *holy covenant* (*covenant*), *abomination of desolation*,[20] *sanctuary fortress*[21] (I mark *sanctuary fortress* like I mark every reference to the Jews' temple), *the regular sacrifice*,[22] and *the end time*.[23] (You may have already marked all the

---

* This is only a small portion of the section on the history of Israel in the *New Inductive Study Bible* (Harvest House). This portion covers the Persian Period through the Period of Roman Rule. If you would like to read the entire section on Israel's history refer to the *NISB*.

references to *the end time,* but make sure you didn't miss any.) Be sure that you marked every reference to the *king of the North* (Antiochus IV Epiphanes).

DAY SIX

Read Daniel 11:21-35 again. List in your notebook everything you learn from noting the references to the king of the North (Antiochus IV Epiphanes).

There are two different groups or types of people mentioned in Daniel 11:29-35. List in your notebook what you learn about each group.

Record the theme of Daniel 11 on the DANIEL AT A GLANCE chart.

DAY SEVEN

Store in your heart: Daniel 11:32b—"but the people who know their God will display strength and take action." (I included the NAS text because I feel it is a good translation.)

Read and discuss: Daniel 11:21-35.

QUESTIONS FOR DISCUSSION OR INDIVIDUAL STUDY

∾ In the light of history, who fulfilled Daniel 11:3,4?

   a. How do the prophecies of Daniel 2:39; 7:6; 8:21,22; and 11:3,4 relate to one another?

   b. What is the significance of the four wings and heads, the four horns, and the four points of the compass?

c. What two generals of Greece played a significant role in the history of Israel? How are they referred to in Daniel 11?

ॐ Which of these kingdoms was ruled over by Antiochus IV Epiphanes?

ॐ What do you learn from Daniel 11:21-35 about Antiochus IV Epiphanes? Note how these observations relate to what you read in regard to the history of Israel.

ॐ What do you learn from marking the key words: *holy covenant (covenant), abomination of desolation, sanctuary fortress, the regular sacrifice,* and *the end time*?

ॐ What do you see as a contrast between the two different groups of people mentioned in Daniel 11:29-35?

ॐ What can you learn from these groups about yourself and how you are to live?

ॐ What do you learn from the verse you are to store in your heart this week? Why is it a good verse to memorize? What would you have to do to fulfill it?

THOUGHT FOR THE WEEK

Antiochus IV Epiphanes was a forerunner of the one who will come as *the* Antichrist, the man of lawlessness, the beast of Revelation 13. A forerunner always gives insight into the one who is to follow. What the Word of God records about this man and about this period of time is for our learning and our admonition upon whom the end of the ages has come.

So what can we learn? First, we see that in times of political distress we need to remember that God is sovereign, and we are to fear and respect Him alone. We are not to forsake the Word of God—the covenant of God—for the sake of political expediency. We are not to put our trust in man, nor are we to fear man. The fear of man always brings a snare in our relationship with God!

Instead, we need to know God and His Word intimately so that we are not swayed by the smooth words of those who do not fear or honor God in their lives. Words must be backed by actions; while many may say, "Lord, Lord," it will mean nothing if they are not doers of the Word of God.

Whether we face flaming furnaces, lions' dens, captivity, or swords, we are to remain faithful to our God— even at the threat of losing our lives.

We also need to remember that since we have been given insight into the times, we need to share our insights and give understanding to others when we have the opportunity.

O Beloved, I commend you for your diligence in doing this study and in getting to know your God better. As you know, what you have disciplined yourself to do will not only strengthen you, it will help you to take action and make an impact on your world. Remember, He is coming and His reward is with Him to give to every one of us according to our deeds (Revelation 22:12).

GOD'S BLUEPRINT
ON THE ANTICHRIST

DAY ONE

Read Daniel 11:36–12:13. Mark *end*[24] and *end of time*[25] (or *end time*[26]) in the same way you marked *end of time* previously. Although you marked time phrases two weeks ago, make sure you didn't miss any.

As you read, remember that what you are reading is part of the vision given to Daniel in chapters 10 and 11. Look at Daniel 10:14 to refresh your memory. The phrase *latter days* in the Hebrew is literally "end of the days," so mark *latter days*[27] the same way you marked *end of time* in Daniel 11 and 12.

Finally, list everything you learn from marking every reference to the *end* in these chapters.

DAY TWO

Read Daniel 11:36-45. Mark every reference to the king, including the pronouns which refer to him. Think about the information the text gives you on this king. As you read, locate the geographical references mentioned in the text on the map on page 98.

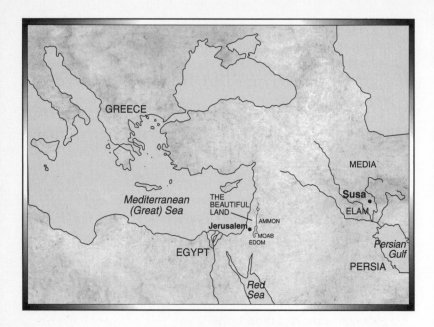

DAY THREE

Make a list of what you see about the king from Daniel 11:36-45. It is interesting that from Daniel 11:36 on, there is no historical record of a literal fulfillment of this king as there is for the previous kings mentioned in Daniel 11:1-35.

DAY FOUR

Read Daniel 12. Mark every reference to *Michael* (including pronouns), and note what he is going to do and why. Also mark every reference to *the holy people* (Daniel's people, the Jews), such as *the sons of your people*[28] or *your people.*[29] Also include any pronouns and synonyms. Also mark every reference to *those who have insight.*[30]

DAY FIVE

Read Daniel 11:45–12:13 once again. Daniel 12:1 begins with the time phrase, "Now at that time."[31] But what time is it referring to? Look at the context—the verse immediately preceding 12:1. Record your insights in your notebook. You also might want to do the same in your Bible.

Now note what is going to happen "at that time" and list your observations. Tomorrow we'll look at some cross-references that will give us further insights into this time.

DAY SIX

Today read Daniel 11:45–12:13 again, but this time read the passage aloud. Then review your notes from yesterday.

Now, look up the following cross-references, checking the context of the verse by reading the verses in parenthesis. Note why or how these verses relate to the same time period as that of Daniel 11:45–12:13. If you agree that they refer to the same period of time, record the cross-references in the margin of your Bible beside the appropriate verses in the Daniel passage: Matthew 24:21 (Matthew 24:15-31); Mark 13:19 (Mark 13:14-27); Joel 2:1,2. We'll do a more in-depth study of these passages next week which you won't want to miss! (By the way, the next study book you ought to do is the one on Revelation—*Behold, Jesus Is Coming!*)

DAY SEVEN

 Store in your heart: Daniel 12:1.
Read and discuss: Daniel 11:36–12:13.

QUESTIONS FOR DISCUSSION OR INDIVIDUAL STUDY

∽ What do you learn about the king of Daniel 11:36-45?

   a. What is his character like?

   b. How long will he prosper?

   c. Whom will he regard and/or honor?

   d. Who will collide with him at the end time? (It would be good to have a map on the board so you can locate the countries he will come into direct conflict with and those who will escape his hand.)

   e. What will be this king's relationship to "the Beautiful Land"?

   f. Where will he pitch his tents?

   g. What will his end be like?

∽ What did you learn from marking the references *end, end of time,* or *end time* in Daniel 11:36–12:13?

   a. How does what you noted compare with what Daniel 11:35 says about the end time?

   b. How concealed and sealed up do you think the book of Daniel is? What is the significance of your answer?

∽ What did you learn about the "time of distress such as never occurred since there was a nation until that time"?

   a. What is the connection between the king of Daniel 11:36-45 and this time?

   b. What is going to happen to Daniel's people at that time?

c. Will everyone be rescued or only a certain group?

d. What do you learn from the references you looked up in Matthew 24:15-31 and Mark 13:14-27?

e. What do you learn from looking up Joel 2:1,2?

∾ What do you learn from Daniel 12 about those who have insight?

a. With whom are they contrasted?

b. How does this compare with those who had insight in the days of Antiochus IV Epiphanes in Daniel 11:29-35?

∾ What insights have you gained during these 12 weeks of study?

a. What kind of responsibility does this place on you? With whom?

b. How interested do you think people are in this subject?

c. How could you use this in presenting the gospel to

1) a Jew?

2) a Gentile?

d. What will be yours if you are faithful to share the things you have learned? What if you don't share?

∾ How is what you're learning going to affect the way you live?

THOUGHT FOR THE WEEK

The Bible tells us that, although many antichrists have arisen, *the* Antichrist is yet to come. Many of us believe he will be personified in the king described in Daniel 11:36-45—a prophecy which has not been literally fulfilled as of this writing. When this king comes into the fulness of his power, there will come a time of distress on this earth such as has never been since there was a nation. The world situation is going to get worse, not better. And more so as the end times approach. The question is, "Are we prepared for the days that are going to precede this time?" We will cover this in more depth in our last lesson.

The book of Daniel was to be sealed up until the end of time. Is it sealed up now or can it be understood? What do you think about Daniel and his prophecies after these past 12 weeks of study? What does that mean in relation to the times?

THE LAST 3½ YEARS
BEFORE MESSIAH COMES

చించించి

DAY ONE

Read through Daniel 12 again. Give careful attention to the words you have marked. In your notebook, list all that is going to happen to "the sons of your people."[32] Note how long it is going to be until "the end of these wonders." How long is it going to be until they finish shattering the power of the "holy people"? Think about Daniel 12:1 and the time of distress in relation to Daniel 12:7. Remember, in biblical reckoning, time, times, and half a time is 3½ years or 1260 days because the biblical calendar has 360 days in a year. What is the relationship between these verses? Record your insights in your notebook.

Now note the time frame connected with the regular sacrifice being abolished and the abomination of desolation being set up.

DAY TWO

Read Daniel 12 again today. Review what you learned last week regarding the "time of distress such as never occurred since there was a nation until that time." You have already looked up Matthew 24:15-31; Mark 13:14-27; and Joel 2:1,2, but read these passages again to refresh your memory. Note what happens during this period of time.

Who are the ones singled out in Matthew 24 and Mark 13 who tell of a great tribulation such as has not occurred since the beginning of the world until now, nor ever shall occur? For whom are those days cut short? Matthew 24 says this is spoken of by Daniel the prophet. Where? Record your insights on these questions in your notebook.

DAY THREE

Considering all you have observed in Daniel, especially Daniel 12, I believe it will be very profitable for you to take the time to compare Scripture with Scripture. Be careful not to get overwhelmed or bogged down with things you don't understand. Instead, simply look for any similarities in what you have seen about the king of Daniel 11:36-45, the time of distress, and the events surrounding Daniel's people in Daniel 12.

Look up 2 Thessalonians 2:1-12. Mark every reference to *the man of lawlessness*,[33] including synonyms and pronouns. Then, in your notebook, make a list of what you learn about him.

DAY FOUR

Continuing where we left off yesterday, read Daniel 12 again and then read Revelation 13:3-8. Mark every reference to the beast in Revelation 13 and then list in your notebook all you learn about him. Note how he is described, what he does, to whom, why, and what happens as a result. Watch for and mark references to time, then note how these compare with Daniel 12.

DAY FIVE

Now, let's take all you have seen this week, especially in the cross-references, and compare it with Daniel's blueprint for prophecy.

Considering what you observed in Revelation 13 and 2 Thessalonians 2 regarding the beast (the man of lawlessness) and what you observed regarding the time of distress mentioned in Daniel 12:1, Matthew 24, Mark 13, and Joel 2, where do these events fit into the prophecy of the statue in Daniel 2? At what part of the statue? Write out your answer and your reasoning in your notebook. Then do the same for Daniel 7:24-26.

DAY SIX

Today, consider where Daniel 9:27 fits into what you observed in Revelation 13, 2 Thessalonians 2, Matthew 24, and Daniel 12. Record your insights in your notebook.

Now study the chart PROPHETIC OVERVIEW OF DANIEL (page 125). Note the relationship of the prophecies of Daniel 2, 7, 8, 9, 11, and 12. This chart represents prophecy given by God through dreams and visions to Nebuchadnezzar and Daniel. Every prophetic event you will ever study (from the time of Nebuchadnezzar through the coming of our Lord Jesus Christ) will fit somewhere within the scope of Daniel's prophecy.

Record the theme of Daniel 12 on the DANIEL AT A
GLANCE chart and fill in the rest of the chart according to
what you have seen. Also note any other insights that you
glean on Daniel and God, as well as any LFLs that you can
apply to your life.

While much of Daniel may still be a mystery, think
of the beginning you have made—the solid foundation of
observation you have laid. Now you have a sure word
of prophecy to build on, my friend. I am proud of you
in the Lord for persevering.

DAY SEVEN

    Store in your heart: Daniel 12:3.
Read and discuss: Daniel 12.

QUESTIONS FOR DISCUSSION OR INDIVIDUAL STUDY

∾ In light of all you have studied this week, what period
of time does Daniel 12 deal with?

a. What relationship do you see between Daniel 12:1, 7,
and 11? Explain.

b. What parallel do you see between this time and the
other passages you have looked up? In your discussion cover them one by one.

Joel 2:1,2
Matthew 24:15-21
Mark 13:14-27
2 Thessalonians 2:1-12
Revelation 13:3-8
Revelation 19:11-16,19,20
Daniel 2:40-45

Daniel 7:24-26

Daniel 9:27

∾ Discuss the chart PROPHETIC OVERVIEW OF DANIEL on page 125.

a. How is it a blueprint for prophecy?

b. Note how and where chapters 7, 8, 9, 11, and 12 explain the big picture of the statue Nebuchadnezzar dreamed about.

c. How would knowing these prophecies have helped the Jews living during and after Daniel's time be prepared for what they experienced?

∾ According to Daniel's prophetic picture, there are only four major kingdoms before the stone crushes the statue and the kingdom of God is set up.

a. What does this tell you must happen in respect to world powers before Jesus comes? Discuss what you learned about the fourth kingdom (Daniel 7:23).

b. How does the fourth kingdom compare with the other three kingdoms and what is the extent of its power in the last 3½ years?

c. How does this compare with Revelation 13:7,8?

∾ What insights have you gleaned in your study of Daniel in respect to:

a. prophecy

b. living as a man or woman of God—a person of high esteem in the eyes of God

c. God Himself

∾ How is this study going to affect the way you live? How you order the affairs of your life? How you spend your time?*

THOUGHT FOR THE WEEK

There is "a prince"—a ruler who is yet to come. Daniel 9:27 tells us he will make a covenant with "the many" for seven years, thus fulfilling and completing the prophecy of Daniel 9:24-27. The seventy weeks of Daniel will finally come to pass. In the middle of those seven years, the final week, the covenant made by the prince apparently will be broken, the regular sacrifice will be stopped, and the abomination of desolation will then be set up in the holy place.

This will take place in the days of the ten kings and the little horn that comes up among them as we learned in Daniel 7. The little horn of Daniel 7 will then shatter the power of God's holy people, the Jews, as he devours the whole earth, treads it down, and crushes it.

As head of the revived fourth kingdom, coming out of the ten kings (the ten toes of the statue), this little horn will subdue all others, walk into the holy place of the Jews' temple in Jerusalem, and declare himself to be God (2 Thessalonians 2:4).

However, 3½ years after this prince (the man of lawlessness) makes his move, he will suddenly be brought to an end and no one will help him. Then complete destruction, one that is decreed, will be poured out on him. And the saints of the Highest One will be given the sovereignty, the

___

* If you want to pursue your study of prophecy may I recommend you study the New Inductive Study Series on Revelation: *Behold, Jesus Is Coming!* and the study on 1 and 2 Thessalonians, *Standing Firm in These Last Days.* (Both are published by Harvest House Publishers.)

dominion, and the greatness of all the kingdoms under the whole heaven.

The King of kings will have come. His kingdom will be an everlasting one and all dominions will serve and obey Him. Daniel will be raised from the dead and receive his allotted portion at the end of the age, and great will be the reward of this man of high esteem.

What will people think when you share all this with them? The wicked will continue to act wickedly and will not understand, but those who have insight will understand. *Share, Beloved, share.* Share in word and in deed. Be as Daniel whose enemies could find nothing to accuse him of before his peers or before his king. Daniel was faithful and no negligence or corruption was found in him. The only way Daniel's enemies could trap him was to bring forth laws that Daniel could not abide by if he was going to be true to God.

May man's only accusation against you be in the same arena—with regard to the law of his God. Stand firm, O man, O woman of high esteem, and take action. I'll be right there beside you!

MAJOR EVENTS IN ISRAEL'S HISTORY

Taken from the *NISB*

The Persian Period
(539 to 331 B.C.)

When the Medes and the Persians conquered Babylon in 539 B.C., they became the predominant world power in Babylon's stead. Daniel 5 records this invasion.

Approximately 175 years before Cyrus (the king of Persia) was born, Isaiah prophesied that God would raise up Cyrus to perform His desire (Isaiah 44:28). Second Chronicles 36:22,23 records the fulfillment of God's plan: Cyrus issued a decree allowing the exiles of Judah to return to Jerusalem and rebuild their temple. Just as Jeremiah had prophesied (Jeremiah 29:10; Daniel 9:2), exactly 70 years from the time of Babylon's first attack on Jerusalem, the Israelites were allowed to return to their land.

The group which returned is referred to in Scripture as the *remnant*. *Diaspora*, the Greek word for scattering, became the term used to describe the Jews who remained in exile among the nations.

The book of Ezra records the return of the remnant and the building of the *second temple* during the time of Haggai and Zechariah. The book of Nehemiah records the rebuilding of the walls of Jerusalem. Nehemiah and Ezra were contemporaries. Ezra is referred to as a *scribe*.

The book of Malachi records the last Old Testament prophecy given by God. After this prophecy God did not inspire canonical Scripture again for 400 years.

This 400 years of silence which followed the book of Malachi is called the *intertestament period*. Although God was silent in that He did not speak through His prophets during this time, the events of these 400 years testify to the fulfillment of much that was written by Daniel the prophet.

These years could be divided into three periods: the Greek, the Maccabean, and the beginning of the Roman period.

∾∾∾∾

The Greek Period
(331 to 63 B.C.)

The Greek period encompasses four different rulerships over Jerusalem, including the Maccabean rule.

∾∾∾∾

Under Alexander the Great
(331 to 323 B.C.)

As the Persian Empire grew and threatened the security of the city-states of Greece, Philip of Macedonia sought to consolidate Greece in an effort to resist attack from Persia.

In 336 B.C. Philip was murdered, and his son, Alexander, who was about 20 years old, became king over the Greek Empire. Within two years Alexander set out to conquer Persia, whose empire now extended westward as far as Asia Minor (modern-day Turkey).

Over the next two years Alexander conquered the territory from Asia Minor to Pakistan and to Egypt, which included the land of the Jews. Although the account is not universally accepted by other historians, Josephus, a Jewish historian who lived about A.D. 37–100, wrote that as Alexander marched into Jerusalem he was met by Jaddua and other Jewish priests dressed in their priestly garments and by the people of Jerusalem wearing white robes.

In a dream Jaddua had been told to put wreaths on the city walls in order to greet Alexander. Alexander also had a dream which coincided with this event. When Alexander was escorted into Jerusalem and shown the prophecy in Daniel 8, which described the destruction of the Medo-Persian Empire by a large horn on a goat (which represented Greece), Alexander felt the prophecy pertained to him and offered the Jews whatever they wanted. Alexander treated the Jews well and did not harm Jerusalem or their rebuilt temple.

When Alexander built the city of Alexandria in Egypt, he encouraged many Jews to settle there in order to help populate the city. Whenever Alexander conquered an area he established Greek cities and colonies, bringing in his Greek culture, ideas, and language. His goal was to consolidate his empire through a common way of life and thinking which became known as *Hellenization*. *Koine Greek* became the common language in the countries ruled by Greece and continued to be the primary language of civilization through the time of Christ. The New Testament was written in Koine Greek.

By 331 B.C. Alexander had conquered Persia. He and his war-weary army returned to Babylon in 323 B.C. When Alexander, one of the greatest military leaders in history, returned to Babylon, history tells us he sat down and wept because there were no more territories to conquer. He died in Babylon in 323 B.C. at the age of 33.

Because Alexander the Great died without an appointed heir, his kingdom fell into chaos. After 22 years of struggle among his generals, it was divided among four of them: Lysimachus, Cassander, Ptolemy I Soter, and Seleucus I Nicator.

The Division of Alexander the Great's Empire			
Lysimachus	**Cassander**	**Ptolemy I Soter**	**Seleucus I Nicator**
took	took	took	took
Thrace and Bithynia	Macedonia	Egypt	Syria

Ptolemy I Soter and Seleucus I Nicator began a succession of competing dynasties for which the land of Israel became a pawn.

∽∾∽∾∽∾

Under the Ptolemies of Egypt
(323 to 204 B.C.)

Ptolemy I Soter, who took Egypt, was given Jerusalem and Judea. The Jews fared well; they were allowed to govern themselves and practice their religion without interference. Under his leadership Jews were permitted to go to Egypt. Some Jews were invited to go to Alexandria and become scholars. The Ptolemies moved Egypt's capital from Memphis to Alexandria and made it the center of learning and commerce. There the Jews were encouraged to use the Greek library, at that time the most extensive and best in the world. As a result many were caught up in philosophy and logic and drank deeply from the cup of Hellenism.

It is believed that Ptolemy II Philadelphus commissioned the translation of the Pentateuch into the Koine Greek. The Greek translation of the entire Old Testament, eventually completed about 100 B.C., was referred to as the *Septuagint* (meaning 70), or abbreviated as the *LXX*. Many of the New Testament writers quoted from the Septuagint.

Other writings produced during this intertestament period are the *Apocrypha*, the *Pseudepigrapha*, and the *Qumran Scrolls* (also called the *Dead Sea Scrolls*). The *Apocrypha* are composed of a variety of writings, including apocalyptic, wisdom, and historical literature. It is from the apocryphal book of First Maccabees that historians gained insight into the period from the Maccabean revolt through the time of John Hyrcanus. The Apocrypha were included in the Septuagint, although they were not part of the Hebrew Scriptures.

The *Pseudepigrapha* are a collection of writings even more extensive than the Apocrypha, but scholars cannot entirely agree on which writings comprise this group. These writings are attributed to noted people such as Adam, Abraham, Enoch, Ezra, and Baruch—but scholars agree that these claims are not authentic.

The *Qumran* or *Dead Sea Scrolls* were manuscripts apparently written or copied between 200 B.C. and A.D. 70 by a Jewish religious sect called *Essenes*. The particular community of Essenes who lived close to the Dead Sea seem to have practiced celibacy and a strictly disciplined communal lifestyle, separating themselves from others. The Dead Sea Scrolls describe the lives and beliefs of this group which lived in the last two centuries before Christ; they also include the oldest known manuscripts of the Old Testament. The scrolls are so named because they were hidden and preserved in some caves near an archaeological excavation called Khirbet Qumran on the western side of the Dead Sea.

∾∾∾∾

Under the Seleucid Kings of Syria
(204 to 165 B.C.)

Those ruling Syria, referred to as the kings of the north in Daniel 11, wanted the beautiful land of Israel. When Antiochus III the Great conquered Ptolemy V Epiphanes of Egypt, Jerusalem and Judea were brought under Syrian dominance.

During this period the land of Israel was sectored into Judea, Samaria, Galilee, Perea, and Trachonitis.

After gaining dominance over the Jews, Antiochus was defeated by the Romans and ended up having to pay Rome a large sum of money for a period of years. To make sure he complied, Rome held his son, Antiochus IV, hostage in Rome.

Antiochus III the Great was succeeded by his son Seleucus IV Philopator, who ruled from 187–175 B.C. In 175 B.C. Antiochus IV Epiphanes (the son who had been held hostage in Rome) usurped the throne by killing his brother. He ruled until 163 B.C. He was called *Epiphanes*, which means "manifest" or "splendid."

Until this period in Israel's history, the priesthood had been a matter of birthright and the office was held for life. However, during his reign Antiochus IV Epiphanes sold the priesthood to Jason, the brother of the high priest. Jason also paid Antiochus a high price in order to build a Greek gymnasium near the temple. During this time many Jews were lured into a Hellenistic way of life. All this brought a great conflict among the orthodox Jews and the "Hellenistic" Jews.

The conflict was heightened when Antiochus IV Epiphanes sought to take the throne of Egypt but was rebuffed by Rome. Because of that and because of what he surmised as a revolt in the priesthood, Antiochus unleashed his anger on those Jews who wouldn't curry his favor or fully adopt Hellenism. He was determined to destroy Judaism. Circumcision was forbidden; those who disobeyed were put to death. Copies of the law were desecrated with heathen symbols or burned, while anyone found with a copy of the law was to be put to death. The Jews were also forbidden to celebrate the Sabbath. Then Antiochus sacrificed a pig on the altar in the temple and erected a statue of Zeus, an abomination of desolation, in the holy place (Daniel 11:31).

Finally, Antiochus sent his officers throughout the land to compel Jews to make sacrifices to Zeus.

The Maccabean Period
(165 to 63 B.C.)

When Antiochus IV Epiphanes' officer arrived in the village of Modein (which lies halfway between Jerusalem and Joppa) and commanded the aged priest Mattathias to make a sacrifice to Zeus, the officer didn't know it was the last official duty he would perform in his life. As Mattathias refused, a younger Jew stepped forward to take his place. When he did, a furious Mattathias plunged his knife not only into the Jewish volunteer but also into the Syrian officer. Mattathias fled with his five sons to the hills…and the Maccabean revolt, led by Mattathias' third son, nick-named Maccabeus (the Hammerer), began.

Three years after Antiochus IV Epiphanes defiled the temple, the Jews recaptured Jerusalem. They removed the statue of Zeus and refurbished the temple and reinstituted Jewish sacrifices. On December 25 the Jews celebrated with a feast of dedication (John 10:22), which from then on became the annual feast of lights or Hanukkah.

Thus began what is referred to as the *Hasmonean Dynasty* as the descendants of Mattathias ruled Israel until Rome conquered Jerusalem in 63 B.C.

When Simon, the last surviving son of Mattathias, was murdered, Simon's son, John Hyrcanus, named himself priest and king. He ruled from 134–104 B.C. He destroyed the Samaritan temple on Mount Gerizim, and from that time on the Jews had no dealings with the Samaritans.

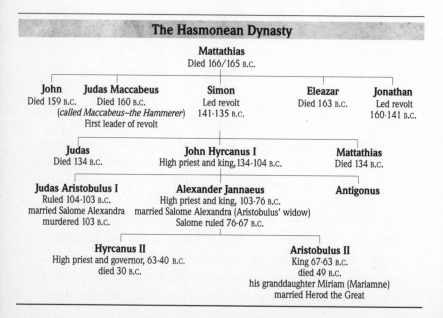

The Hasmonean Dynasty

Mattathias
Died 166/165 B.C.

John	Judas Maccabeus	Simon	Eleazar	Jonathan
Died 159 B.C.	Died 160 B.C. *(called Maccabeus–the Hammerer)* First leader of revolt	Led revolt 141-135 B.C.	Died 163 B.C.	Led revolt 160-141 B.C.

Judas	John Hyrcanus I	Mattathias
Died 134 B.C.	High priest and king, 134-104 B.C.	Died 134 B.C.

Judas Aristobulus I	Alexander Jannaeus	Antigonus
Ruled 104-103 B.C. married Salome Alexandra murdered 103 B.C.	High priest and king, 103-76 B.C. married Salome Alexandra (Aristobulus' widow) Salome ruled 76-67 B.C.	

Hyrcanus II	Aristobulus II
High priest and governor, 63-40 B.C. died 30 B.C.	King 67-63 B.C. died 49 B.C. his granddaughter Miriam (Mariamne) married Herod the Great

After that Hyrcanus moved southeast and conquered the land of the Idumeans, who came from the ancient kingdom of Edom. The peoples of this land were given the choice of emigrating or converting to Judaism. This was the land of Herod the Great, who would someday become Rome's appointed king of the Jews.

During the reign of John Hyrcanus, the *Pharisees,* a religious sect of the Jews, arose from the Hasidim. The *Hasidim,* a militant religious community dedicated to the obedience of the law and the worship of God, began around 168 B.C. and was active during the Maccabean revolt. The word *Pharisee* means "separated one" and was probably used to describe these men because they separated themselves from the strong influence of Hellenism. During New Testament times the majority of the scribes were Pharisees.

Doctrinally the Pharisees viewed the entire Old Testament as authoritative; however, they also accepted the oral tradition as equally authoritative. To the Pharisee, to study the law was true worship. They believed in life after death, the resurrection, and the existence of angels and demons. Although the Pharisees taught that the way to God was through keeping the law, they were more liberal in their interpretation of the law than were the Sadducees. The Pharisees represented the largest religious sect, but their numbers declined when they fell into John Hyrcanus' disfavor.

The *Sadducees,* a smaller religious sect comprised mostly of the upper classes, were often of the priestly line and were usually more wealthy than the Pharisees. For the most part the Pharisees were of the middle-class merchants and tradesmen. The Sadducees accepted only the *Torah* (the first five books of the Old Testament) as authoritative.

While they were rigid in the observance of the law and held to its literal interpretation, they denied divine providence, the resurrection, life after death, the existence of angels and demons, and any reward or punishment after death. They opposed the oral law as obligatory or binding and were materialistic.

The Sadducees controlled the temple and its services. However, because the Sadducees leaned toward Hellenism, they were unpopular with the majority of the Jewish populace.

Aristobulus I, who succeeded his father, John Hyrcanus, married Salome Alexandra. However, when Aristobulus died, Salome married his brother Alexander Jannaeus, who became high priest and king in 103 B.C. This marriage created many enemies for Alexander Jannaeus because the high priest was to marry only a virgin.

When he died in 76 B.C., his wife, Salome Alexandra, took the throne, but as a woman she could not hold the office of high priest, so her oldest son, Hyrcanus II, assumed that position.

Civil war broke out when Salome died, because her youngest son, Aristobulus II, who was supported by the Sadducees, sought to take the throne from Hyrcanus II. He was willing to give up that position, but Antipater (an Idumean and the father of Herod the Great) befriended Hyrcanus and persuaded him to seek outside help in order to regain his position as the rightful heir. Hyrcanus' forces came against Aristobulus and defeated him. He had to flee and made the temple in Jerusalem his fortress, but he was besieged by Hyrcanus' forces.

Early in this period the Hasmoneans had made a treaty with Rome in order to keep Syria, their northern neighbors, in check. Now the Roman army under Scaurus was in

Syria because Seleucid rule had collapsed. Scaurus heard about the civil war in Judea and went there. Both Aristobulus and Hyrcanus sought his help. Scaurus sided with Aristobulus and had the siege lifted from Jerusalem, but the fighting continued. An appeal was made to the Roman general Pompey, who said he would settle the dispute and urged them to keep peace until he arrived. However, Aristobulus went back to Jerusalem to prepare resistance, which caused Rome's support to turn to Hyrcanus. Pompey arrived and took Aristobulus and his family captive, besieging the city for three months.

The Period of Roman Rule
(63 B.C. to A.D. 70)

In 63 B.C. Pompey conquered Jerusalem and with some of his soldiers walked into the holy of holies. Although they didn't touch any of the furnishings, they alienated the Jews, who never forgave Pompey. About 12,000 Jews died during this Roman siege of Jerusalem, a supposed attempt to settle a civil war.

Rome broke up the Hasmonean dynasty and their territory. Judea was now reduced to smaller borders, and its independence was lost. It was now a territory of Rome. Hyrcanus II could be the rightful priest but not king. He was now under the governor of Syria, a Roman province. Scaurus was appointed governor. Aristobulus and many Jews were taken to Rome. Not much later Gabinius, a Roman governor of Syria, took control. He entrusted the temple to Hyrcanus and changed the government of Judea.

The Jewish state was divided into five districts governed by a council that remained under the jurisdiction of the governor of Syria; Hyrcanus, the high priest, was made ruler over Jerusalem. Antipater was his chief magistrate.

The high priest presided over the *Sanhedrin,* a 71-member council comprised of both Sadducees and Pharisees, which governed the Jews under the authority of Rome. Although the Sanhedrin seemed to have autonomy in the matters of the civil and criminal government of the Jews, apparently the Sanhedrin was not allowed to put people to death without the permission of the Roman procurator. The Sanhedrin is often referred to as "the council" in the Gospels and Acts.

In 55 B.C. three men—Pompey, Crassus (the governor of Syria), and Julius Caesar—controlled Rome. Crassus, considering himself another Alexander the Great, set out to conquer the world. However, just before this he stole the treasures from the temple in Jerusalem. Crassus and his army were later destroyed by the Parthians.

Parthia, southeast of the Caspian Sea and part of the Persian Empire, had been conquered by Alexander the Great. But Rome would not conquer them until A.D. 114.

After Crassus' death, Julius Caesar took Italy and then set out to destroy Pompey. Pompey fled to Egypt, where he was assassinated. During this time Antipater supported Caesar, so out of gratitude Caesar gave him the official title of Procurator of Judea.

Antipater made his son Phasael governor of Judea and his son Herod governor of Galilee. Hyrcanus II remained high priest, although Antipater and his two sons robbed him of his authority.

In 44 B.C. Caesar was murdered by Brutus and Cassius. Civil war broke out in Rome. Cassius took control of the east. Because of the instability of Rome, Hyrcanus' rivals made a bid for power.

When Antipater was murdered in 43 B.C. Antigonus, Aristobulus' son (who was supported by the Parthians), invaded the country.

At that time Herod came to the aid of Hyrcanus, who out of gratitude gave Herod a beautiful woman named Miriam. They were not married until five years later.

After that Brutus and Cassius were defeated by Mark Antony and Caesar's nephew Octavian (who would later become Caesar Augustus). Mark Antony became ruler of the east. In 40 B.C., when the Parthians invaded Palestine, Herod fled to Rome.

That year, at the urging of Antony and Octavian, Herod was made king of the Jews. It took him three years to rid the area of the Parthians and establish his rule in Judea. Just before laying siege to Jerusalem, Herod married Miriam (also called Mariamne), hoping that his marriage into the Hasmonean family would make him more acceptable to the Jews.

In 20 B.C. Herod began rebuilding the temple. The one built by Zerubbabel after the Babylonian exile was so pitifully small in comparison to the first temple that Herod was determined to make it larger and more magnificent than Solomon's. Although the temple itself was completed in a year-and-a-half, the construction and decoration of its outer courts continued for years, so in A.D 26 the Jews would say, "It took forty-six years to build this temple" (John 2:20).

Herod, whose people (the Idumeans) had been forced to convert to Judaism under John Hyrcanus, was only a Jew in practice when he lived in Judea. Although Rome gave

Herod the title "King of the Jews," he was never accepted by those he ruled over.

Then "in the days of Herod the king, behold, magi from the east arrived in Jerusalem, saying, 'Where is He who has been born King of the Jews?'" (Matthew 2:1,2).

The true King had come...the Ruler who would shepherd God's people Israel (Matthew 2:6).

Herod died in 4 B.C. But those living in Judea and Galilee saw a great light and heard with their own ears the voice of God, the King of kings.

The 400 years of silence had been broken.

Prophetic Overview of Daniel

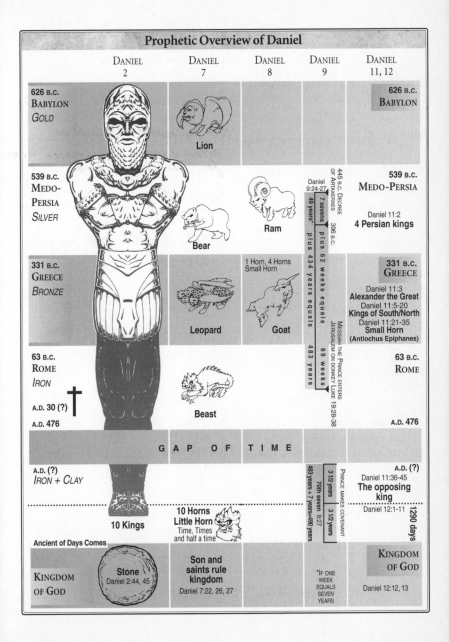

	DANIEL 2	DANIEL 7	DANIEL 8	DANIEL 9	DANIEL 11, 12
626 B.C. BABYLON *GOLD*		Lion			**626 B.C. BABYLON**
539 B.C. MEDO-PERSIA *SILVER*		Bear	Ram	Daniel 9:24-27	**539 B.C. MEDO-PERSIA** Daniel 11:2 **4 Persian kings**
331 B.C. GREECE *BRONZE*		Leopard	1 Horn, 4 Horns Small Horn — Goat		**331 B.C. GREECE** Daniel 11:3 **Alexander the Great** Daniel 11:5-20 **Kings of South/North** Daniel 11:21-35 **Small Horn** (Antiochus Epiphanes)
63 B.C. ROME *IRON* A.D. 30 (?) A.D. 476		Beast			**63 B.C. ROME** A.D. 476
			GAP OF TIME		
A.D. (?) *IRON + CLAY*					**A.D. (?)** Daniel 11:36-45 **The opposing king** Daniel 12:1-11
	10 Kings	**10 Horns Little Horn** Time, Times and half a time			
Ancient of Days Comes					
KINGDOM OF GOD	**Stone** Daniel 2:44, 45	**Son and saints rule kingdom** Daniel 7:22, 26, 27		*IF ONE WEEK EQUALS SEVEN YEARS	**KINGDOM OF GOD** Daniel 12:12, 13

445 B.C. DECREE OF ARTAXERXES

Daniel 9:24-27

7 sevens — 49 years

396 B.C.

plus 62 weeks equals

plus 434 years equals

69 weeks

483 years

MESSIAH THE PRINCE ENTERS JERUSALEM ON DONKEY LUKE 19:28-38

PRINCE MAKES COVENANT 9:27

483 years + 7 years=490 years

70th seven

3 1/2 years

3 1/2 years

1290 days

Theme of Daniel:

Author:

Historical
Setting:

Purpose:

Key Words:

SEGMENT DIVISIONS		KINGS/ KINGDOM		CHAPTER THEMES
			1	God allows Daniel to be taken captive, prepares him for service to Neb.
			2	Daniel interprets N's dream
			3	S, M, A into the furnace
			4	
			5	
			6	
			7	
			8	
			9	
			10	
			11	
			12	

NOTES

෴෴

1. KJV: *the high God, the most High*

2. NIV: *wickedness*

3. NIV: *goblets*

4. NIV: also *accessories*

5. NIV: also *I watched, I looked, I continued to watch*
   KJV: *I beheld, I saw*
   NKJV: *I watched, I looked, I saw, I was watching*

6. NIV; KJV; NKJV: These translations do not use *the Highest One*; they use *the Most High*.

7. KJV: "time and times and the dividing of time"
   NKJV: "time and times and half a time"

8. KJV: also *time...the end*
   NKJV: also *time the end*

9. NIV: *the time of wrath*
   KJV: *the last end of the indignation*
   NKJV: *the latter time of the indignation*

10. NIV: *the time of wrath*
    KJV: *the last end of the indignation*
    NKJV: *the latter time of the indignation*

11. KJV: also *time...the end*
    NKJV: also *time the end*

12. KJV: *Thy city*

13. KJV: *Thy holy mountain*

14. KJV; NKJV: also *sins*

15. NIV: *his holy hill*

16. NIV: Uses the word *sevens* instead of *weeks*.

17. KJV: *unto*

18. NIV: *the Anointed One*

19. NIV: *the ruler who will come*
    KJV: *the prince that shall come*

20. NIV: *abomination that causes desolation*
    KJV: *abomination that maketh desolate*

21. NIV: *temple fortress*
    KJV: *sanctuary of strength*

22. NIV; KJV: *the daily sacrifice*
    NKJV: *daily sacrifices*

23. NIV; KJV; NKJV: *the time of the end*

24. NIV: also *fulfilled*
    NKJV: also *fulfillment*

25. NIV; KJV; NKJV: *time of the end*

26. NIV; KJV; NKJV: Translates *end time* as *time of the end.*

27. NIV: *future*

28. KJV: *children of thy people*

29. KJV: *thy people*

30. NIV: *who are wise*
    KJV: *that be wise, the wise*
    NKJV: *who are wise, the wise*

31. NIV; NKJV: *At that time*
    KJV: *And at that time*

32. KJV: *children of thy people*

33. KJV: *that man of sin*
    NKJV: *the man of sin*